Critical Infrastructures Resilience

This text offers comprehensive and principled, yet practical, guidelines to critical infrastructures resilience. Extreme events and stresses, including those that may be unprecedented but are no longer surprising, have disproportionate effects on critical infrastructures and hence on communities, cities, and megaregions.

Critical infrastructures include buildings and bridges, dams, levees, and sea walls, as well as power plants and chemical factories, besides lifeline networks such as multimodal transportation, power grids, communication, and water or wastewater. The growing interconnectedness of natural-built human systems causes cascading infrastructure failures and necessitates simultaneous recovery. This text explores the new paradigm centered on the concept of resilience by approaching the challenges posed by globalization, climate change, and growing urbanization on critical infrastructures and key resources through the combination of policy and engineering perspectives. It identifies solutions that are scientifically credible, data driven, and sound in engineering principles while concurrently informed by and supportive of social and policy imperatives.

Critical Infrastructures Resilience will be of interest to students of engineering and policy.

Auroop Ratan Ganguly is Professor of Civil and Environmental Engineering and Director of the Sustainability and Data Sciences Laboratory at Northeastern University. He has nearly 20 years' total work experience spanning the R&D organizations of Oracle Corporation and a best-of-breed company acquired by Oracle, as a senior scientist at the Oak Ridge National Laboratory, and within academia in multiple roles. His current research is at the intersection of weather or climate extremes and water, infrastructural resilience and homeland security, as well as machine learning, statistics, and nonlinear dynamics. He has led or co-led projects worth about $19 million funded by NSF, NASA, DHS, DOE, DOD, and other agencies.

Udit Bhatia is a PhD student in the Department of Civil and Environmental Engineering at Northeastern University. His research interests include infrastructure resilience, ecosystem recovery, climate, and hydrology. Previously, he served as Assistant Design Engineer (Structures) in MECON Ltd. (Government of India Enterprise). He was the founder of a successful engineering startup, the educational wing of which developed learning modules delivered to students through remote technologies and face-to-face interactions.

Stephen E. Flynn is Professor of Political Science and Founding Director of the Global Resilience Institute at Northeastern University. Dr Flynn served as President of the Center for National Policy and as senior fellow for National Security Studies at the Council on Foreign Relations. He is one of the world's leading experts on critical infrastructure and supply chain security and resilience. He is a member of the Homeland Security Science and Technology Advisory Council.

"The book *Critical Infrastructures Resilience* is a fantastic addition to a knowledge area that is of increasing importance to our society today. At the same time that existing infrastructure is aging and deteriorating, the stresses upon them are increasing because of changing weather patterns and increasing incidence and frequency of extreme events. The authors, respected experts in this area, use this book to fill a knowledge gap, providing fantastic material to allow engineers and public policy professionals to better understand this complex problem and its solutions."

– Lucio Soibelman, Professor of Civil and Environmental
Engineering, University of Southern California

"The resilience of urban communities to natural and anthropogenic hazards depends on the performance of the built environment and on supporting social, economic, and public institutions functioning as integrated systems. This book is timely in light of the growth of urban infrastructure, populations, and economic development in regions that are susceptible natural hazards, such as earthquakes, hurricanes coupled with storm surge, and sea level rise. Coverage includes major areas of concern to urban resilience assessment and risk mitigation: modeling critical infrastructure systems and their interdependencies, probabilistic risk assessment, and development of risk-informed public policy. Written at a time when resilience research is reaching a critical mass, this book is a welcome addition to the literature, providing a unique perspective by leaders in the field of critical infrastructure systems on quantitative urban resilience assessment."

– Bruce R. Ellingwood, Co-director, Center of Excellence for
Risk-Based Community Resilience Planning,
Colorado State University

"Harvey, Irma, Maria—common names for uncommon natural disasters that highlighted how brittle our cities and their infrastructure are. This book guides students and practitioners through the methodologies that can be used to quantify the risk natural and man-made events present to our infrastructure. Those learners will be better prepared to design more resilient cities and communities capable of withstanding increasingly common extreme events."

– Rafael L. Bras, Provost and Executive Vice President
for Academic Affairs, Georgia Institute of Technology

Critical Infrastructures Resilience

Policy and Engineering Principles

Auroop Ratan Ganguly,
Udit Bhatia, and
Stephen E. Flynn

Routledge
Taylor & Francis Group

NEW YORK AND LONDON

First published 2018
by Routledge
605 Third Avenue, New York, NY 10017

and by Routledge
2 Park Square, Milton Park, Abingdon, Oxon, OX14 4RN

First issued in paperback 2021

Routledge is an imprint of the Taylor & Francis Group, an informa business

© 2018 Taylor & Francis

The right of Auroop Ratan Ganguly, Udit Bhatia, and Stephen E. Flynn to be identified as authors of this work has been asserted by them in accordance with sections 77 and 78 of the Copyright, Designs and Patents Act 1988.

Publisher's Note
The publisher has gone to great lengths to ensure the quality of this reprint but points out that some imperfections in the original copies may be apparent.

Library of Congress Cataloging-in-Publication Data
Names: Ganguly, Auroop R., author. | Bhatia, Udit, author. | Flynn, Stephen E., author.
Title: Critical infrastructures resilience : policy and engineering principles / Auroop Ratan Ganguly, Udit Bhatia, and Stephen E. Flynn.
Description: New York, NY : Routledge, 2018. | Includes bibliographical references and index.
Identifiers: LCCN 2017047021 | ISBN 9781498758635 (hardback) | ISBN 9781498758642 (webPDF) | ISBN 9781351649094 (ePub) | ISBN 9781351639576 (Mobipocket/Kindle)
Subjects: LCSH: Infrastructure (Economics)—Protection. | Emergency management—Government policy—United States. | Disasters—Risk assessment. | Organizational resilience. | Public works—United States.
Classification: LCC TA23 .G34 2018 | DDC 363.34—dc23
LC record available at https://lccn.loc.gov/2017047021

Typeset in Times New Roman
by Apex CoVantage, LLC

ISBN 13: 978-1-03-224188-3 (pbk)
ISBN 13: 978-1-4987-5863-5 (hbk)

Auroop Ganguly dedicates this book to three of his biggest fans (even though they may not consider themselves as such): his nephew Rhik and his cousins Deep and Mishtee.

Udit Bhatia dedicates this book to his niece Shravya and his nephew Ayaan.

Stephen Flynn dedicates this book to JoAnn and Christina, the two great loves of his life.

Auroop R. Ganguly
Udit Bhatia
Stephen E. Flynn

August 31, 2017
Boston, Massachusetts, USA

Contents

Detailed Contents

Figures

Tables

About the Authors

Auroop Ratan Ganguly is a Professor of Civil and Environmental Engineering, and Professor by Courtesy of Computer and Information Engineering and also Marine and Environmental Science, at Northeastern University in Boston, Massachusetts. His research and teaching activities encompass hydrology and climate, infrastructures and security, as well as nonlinear dynamics and machine learning. He directs the interdisciplinary Sustainability and Data Sciences Laboratory (SDS Lab), where he develops novel and actionable predictive understanding of climate and hydrological extremes and lifeline infrastructure networks based on hybrid physics-based models and data-driven methods, which in turn draw from artificial intelligence and machine learning, time series and spatial or spatiotemporal statistics, nonlinear dynamics, and network sciences, as well as optimization and econometrics. His SDS Lab aspires to develop fundamental hydrology and climate science understanding, innovate in resilience engineering principles, and develop novel technologies and methods that leverage the power of data, computation, and physics. Prior to his current position at Northeastern, he was at the U.S. Department of Energy's Oak Ridge National Laboratory for seven years in their Computational Sciences and Engineering Division, at Oracle Corporation for five years in their Time Series and Demand Forecasting groups, and at a startup subsequently acquired by Oracle for a year. Prior to that he was at the University of South Florida, Tampa, and the University of Tennessee, Knoxville, as visiting or joint faculty. He has published in *Nature, Nature Climate Change, PNAS, PLOS ONE, Nature's Scientific Reports*, and other interdisciplinary and major disciplinary journals; won best paper awards at highly selective peer-reviewed computer science conferences; and published edited books on Knowledge Discovery from Sensor Data. He currently serves on the editorial board of *Nature's Scientific Reports*, as an associate editor of *ASCE Journal of Computing in Civil Engineering*, and an elected member of the Artificial Intelligence Committee of the American Meteorological Society. He has also served as an associate editor of the journal *Water Resources Research*, published by the American Geophysical Union; edited special issues of *Nonlinear Processes in Geophysics and Intelligent Data Analysis*; and served as organizer or program committee member of multiple peer-reviewed computer science conferences or workshops. His research has been widely cited and he has been quoted in the national and international media. He is a Co-founder and Chief Scientific Adviser at risQ, Inc., an NSF-funded startup, and obtained a PhD from the Department of Civil and Environmental Engineering at the Massachusetts Institute of Technology, both in Cambridge, Massachusetts.

Udit Bhatia is a graduate student in the Department of Civil and Environmental Engineering at Northeastern University, Boston. His research interests include infrastructure resilience, ecosystem recovery, climate, and hydrology. Udit has published journal papers, book chapters, and encyclopedia articles; was selected as excellent youth paper award candidate at the International Conference on Sustainable Infrastructures; and has presented his work at multiple conferences. Prior to joining the PhD program under the supervision of Prof. Auroop Ganguly, he was working in the capacity of Assistant Design Engineer (Structures) in MECON Ltd. (Government of India Enterprise). His research experience includes an internship from the Indian Institute of Technology, Mumbai, as an IRCC Research Internship award recipient, where he was part of the project "Climate Change Impact Assessment on Water Resources of India." He was the founder of a successful engineering startup, the educational wing of which developed learning modules delivered to students through remote technologies and face-to-face interactions. The design wing of the company has worked on the development of architectural solutions for low-cost housing. Udit holds a Bachelor of Technology in Civil Engineering from the National Institute of Technology, Hamirpur, India.

Stephen E. Flynn is a Professor of Political Science and Professor by Courtesy of Civil and Environmental Engineering at Northeastern University. He is also Founding Director of the Global Resilience Institute, and Co-director of the George J. Kostas Research Institute for Homeland Security. Appointed by the U.S. Secretary of Homeland Security, he serves as a member of the Homeland Security Science and Technology Advisory Council (HSSTAC). He served as President of the Center for National Policy and spent a decade as a senior fellow for National Security Studies at the Council on Foreign Relations. He is recognized as one of the world's leading experts on enterprise resilience, critical infrastructure assurance, and transportation and supply chain security and resilience. He holds research affiliations with the Wharton School's Risk Management and Decision Processes Center, and Columbia University's National Center for Disaster Preparedness at the Earth Institute. He received MALD and PhD degrees from the Fletcher School of Law and Diplomacy, Tufts University, in 1990 and 1991, respectively.

Preface

This textbook explores the resilience of critical infrastructures, broadly construed, when subjected to multiple natural and man-made hazards. Of the many sources of global turbulence, the 2017 Global Risk Report published by the World Economic Forum placed "Extreme Weather Events" at the very top both in terms of likelihood and impact. As recent events have highlighted, the salience of the weather extremes risk has become particularly so in coastal and urban regions.

Cities and coastlines are in the crosshairs of climate change and weather extremes. The stakes could not be higher because this is where so much of economic activity and people is concentrated. Hurricanes Katrina and Sandy, record-breaking rainfall in South Carolina, record snow in New England, and the devastation to the Houston metro area wrought by the flooding associated with Hurricane Harvey should be clarion calls to action for the United States. Across the world, major cities from Mumbai and Miami to Jakarta and Shanghai are struggling to come to grips with their growing vulnerability to rising sea level and the associated storm surge risk. Public leaders desperately need support from technical and policy advisers who understand and can help deploy novel engineering and policy approaches that are, in turn, informed by best practices in physical and social sciences. The imperative to engineer coastal cities for regional climate resilience has become global. This book discusses and formalizes creative approaches to the complex challenge of managing the interfaces across coupled natural-built human system of systems. This includes addressing (1) non-stationarity and deep uncertainty, along with complex dependence in space and time, that in combination pose fundamental challenges for climate adaptation at stakeholder-relevant scales and projection horizons; (2) small stresses that percolate across a single infrastructure sector, such as the power grid, or cascade across other lifeline sectors such as liquid fuels, communications, transportation, and water, leading to system-level failures; (3) natural and built infrastructures acting as part of a coupled human-natural system where a catastrophic failure in one will inevitably lead to failure in the other; and (4) the growing connectivity of social institutions as both a current constraint and a potential opportunity to advance adaptation. There is a need to understand and overcome the potential for major shocks to generate domino effects that arise from these interconnections.

Herding cats, swans, and butterflies to confront hell or high water are among the more colorful ways that we might describe efforts to ensure critical infrastructures resilience in the face of weather extremes. Cats are not herd animals, so the phrase "herding cats" describes attempts to bring together entities that are difficult to manage for a specific purpose. Developing resilience of critical infrastructures to weather extremes requires the ability to merge solutions for different challenges: (1) cats refer to both Natural Catastrophe ("Nat Cat") models used in insurance and Catastrophe ("Cat") bonds, and broadly allude to financial incentives that need to be developed to drive resilience efforts; (2) swans are the so-called black swans, or extremely rare and unpredictable events with disproportionate impacts, as well as so-called grey swans, which describe what may be called predictive surprise, or unprecedented but no longer surprising events, and have been used to describe, for example, tropical storms of the future including hurricanes along the U.S. coastline; and (3) butterflies refer to the "butterfly effect" in complex nonlinear dynamical systems, especially in the context of chaos theory, and is used here to convey the complexity of weather and climate, as well as the coupled natural-built human systems impacted by weather and climate. The combined ability to tame complexity, understand unprecedented yet unsurprising extremes, and drive incentive structures and governance models is the key to developing resilience. This book addresses resilience at multiple scales, including community resilience in coastal cities to regional resilience in interconnected urban regions.

The unfortunate reality is that cities, coastlines, and entire nations remain inadequately prepared for the growing array of risks that confront them. Stakeholders such as urban or regional planners, infrastructure owners and operators, and ecosystem or resource managers desperately need to acquire a unified view of the state of a coastal city's infrastructures, and require access to planning and policy tools that can help to guide investment decisions, identify and relieve chokepoints, and determine how to make appropriate trade-offs. This book aspires to introduce students to many of these concepts, with an emphasis on policy-relevant engineering principles. Fundamental research is needed to overcome shortcomings in our current science understanding, engineering principles, and methods or tools by tackling hard questions such as reconciling disparate space-time scales, managing uncertainty that cannot be well handled in existing probabilistic frameworks, characterizing extremes that co-occur and failures that propagate along interconnected systems, and optimizing multiple objectives with uncertain information. We believe the solutions are within reach, if only as a society we care enough to build them. This book will hopefully inspire and enable the next generation of engineers and policy students to address this challenge.

Auroop R. Ganguly
Udit Bhatia
Stephen E. Flynn

August 31, 2017
Boston, Massachusetts, USA

Acknowledgements

An innovative graduate course called "Critical Infrastructure Resilience" was designed and has been offered thrice at Northeastern University in Boston, Massachusetts. The course is offered as CIVE 7110 to engineering and science students and as POLS 7704 to students in social science and policy, taught jointly by Auroop R. Ganguly and Stephen E. Flynn, and offered in a single classroom for both CIVE 7110 and POLS 7704 students. For the recent two offerings, Udit Bhatia has been the primary graduate teaching assistant. The genesis of this textbook came out of teaching the course, and the final contents have evolved significantly given the pace of new developments within this field. We are especially grateful to all the graduate students who willingly embraced a course that stretched them outside the comfort of their academic backgrounds as either civil engineers or political scientists. We also are indebted to the dedicated staff of instructional designers at Northeastern, led by Melanie Kasparian who helped develop the course's extensive online materials. The authors thank Mary Elizabeth ("Lizzy") Warner, who went through the chapters and provided comments.

Auroop R. Ganguly would like to thank his long-suffering yet infinitely patient wife Debashree Bagchi Ganguly; his parents Deepali and Nirmal Kumar Ganguly, without whose inspiration nothing would have been possible; his former doctoral student and current colleague Evan Kodra; the current and former students and postdoctoral associates at his Sustainability and Data Sciences Laboratory (SDS Lab); and his undergraduate, post-master's, and postdoc mentees at the Oak Ridge National Laboratory.

Udit Bhatia would like to thank his parents, Shashi and Krishan Lal Bhatia, and his better half, Mehak Bhatia, who apart from being constant sources of inspiration have been uncompromising supporters. The author is thankful to all his colleagues at the Sustainability and Data Sciences Lab.

Stephen Flynn is particularly grateful to the support from Robbin Peach and George Naccara at the Massachusetts Port Authority and Andre Martecchini and Nasser Brahim at Kleinfelder, who agreed to support the students as they conducted their fieldwork between 2013 and 2016. He also acknowledges the support of his Northeastern University colleague Peter Boynton and his teacher's assistant Andrew MacPherson. Finally, he is indebted to Mitchell Orenstein, former chair of the Political Science Department, and Jerry Hajjar, chair of the Civil and Environmental Engineering Department, for being willing to support a course that stretched traditional interdisciplinary boundaries.

Auroop R. Ganguly
Udit Bhatia
Stephen E. Flynn

August 31, 2017
Boston, Massachusetts, USA

1 Introduction to Critical Infrastructures Resilience

1.1 Introduction

The "Critical Infrastructure Resilience Final Report and Recommendations" by the National Infrastructure Advisory Council (NIAC 2013) starts its executive summary with the following sentences:[1]

> Business and society operate in an increasingly complex world marked by interconnection and interdependence across global networks. This complexity requires that owners and operators of critical infrastructures manage their operational risks in an all-hazards environment across the full spectrum of prevention, protection, response, recovery, and reconstitution activities.

While recognizing that each Critical Infrastructure (CI) sector may operate differently, the report motivates a common definition of Critical Infrastructure Resilience (CIR) for effective governance and policy. The report essentially suggests that CIR is about "delivering the goods" despite disruptions. We note that disruptions could be in the form of acute perturbation (e.g., extreme events such as hurricanes, snowstorms, terror attacks) or stresses that build over time (e.g., droughts, social segregation, aging infrastructures). A correspondence in the journal *Nature* highlighted that resilience has been defined in more than 70 ways, and these definitions are likely to have long-term policy implications to achieve the objective.[2] An operational definition of CIR was proposed by NIAC 2013:

> **Infrastructure resilience** is the ability to reduce the magnitude and/or duration of disruptive events. The effectiveness of a resilient infrastructure or enterprise depends upon its ability to anticipate, absorb, adapt to, and/or rapidly recover from a potentially disruptive event.

To address the similar questions and challenges in critical infrastructures, the risk-based framework has been the tool of choice for engineers and organizations to study threat-impact relationships. For example, in the context of critical infrastructures, the U.S. Department of Homeland Security defines risk as:

> The potential for an unwanted outcome resulting from an incident, event, or occurrence, as determined by its likelihood and the associated consequences.

Risk is influenced by the nature and magnitude of threat or hazard, the vulnerabilities from the threat and hazard, and the consequences that could result.[3]

Risk from an extreme event results from the interaction of hazards (which includes hazardous and/or extreme events) with the vulnerability and exposure of human and natural systems. Changes in both the nature and magnitude of hazards and socioeconomic processes are drivers of hazards, exposure, vulnerability, and hence risk.

Quantitative estimates of risk assessments are obtained using the Probabilistic Risk Assessment (PRA) Framework to estimate the risk by computing real numbers to determine what is the likelihood of occurrence of hazard and the magnitude of the possible adverse consequences. Consequences are expressed numerically and their likelihoods are expressed as probabilities or frequencies. We will discuss PRA in more detail in subsequent chapters.

PRA has been widely used over the last several decades across sectors ranging from basic sciences and engineering to business and government. Risk management has been used as a tool for preserving ecosystems, securing infrastructures, safeguarding cyberinfrastructures, and making financial decisions. While conceptually generic, risk-based investments and preparedness tend to be threat-centric, situation dependent, and system specific. In contrast, proponents of resilience paradigms have attempted to motivate measures and approaches that are threat-agnostic, adaptable to diverse situations, and ubiquitous across systems. Furthermore, while risk approaches may attempt to reduce system perturbations, the resilience paradigm motivates what has been called graceful degradation or allowing either intentional failure or partial component level collapse to reduce the possibility of permanent or system-wide loss of functionality, albeit with rapid recovery times [4,5]. As the following cases illustrate, the benefits of the resilience paradigm beyond risk management may range from crucial to incremental and occasionally even infeasible to achieve.

Case 1: Threat-centric versus threat-agnostic approach. It may indeed be beneficial to embed resilience across the systems in a way that enhances robustness and increases recovery potential for multiple hazards. However, in many cases, deriving co-benefits across multiple types of threats may not be possible and could even be counterproductive. Let us consider floods, earthquakes, and terror attacks. Investments made in emergency management services such as emergency health care, law enforcement, and communication can result in co-benefits across these hazards. However, co-benefits are not always feasible. For example, consider an organization that is planning to invest to secure its high-value assets such as data server buildings and headquarters from external security threats. Enabling such capacities will entail investments in perimeter fencing and anti-theft systems. While these measures will certainly build capacities against the spectrum of security-related threats, contribution of these investments to enable resilience to natural hazards such as floods and earthquakes may be minimal. There are examples where exclusive focus on co-benefits may be counterproductive or even infeasible. For example, National Electrical Code (NEC) guidelines produced by the National Fire Protection Association of the United States require electric installations (such as power breakers and power backups) in buildings to be placed in well-illuminated, easily accessible areas without any obstructions in the working space. To meet these requirements without compromising aesthetics, it has been a common practice to install these units under stairways, in garages, or in basements. However, during a flooding event, these preferred regions may be most susceptible to flooding. FEMA guidelines specify the following:

> Buildings typically respond to an earthquake such that the accelerations at the top of a building can be two or three times stronger than those at the base. Therefore, if flood or storm surge hazards are not present, it is recommended that emergency power equipment and ancillary systems be located at grade since seismic demands will be lower. It is generally not good practice to locate emergency power systems in the basement, since they may be flooded by seismic failure of piping systems. . . . Where both seismic and flood risks exist, critical functions and the equipment needed to support those functions should be located on floor(s) with elevations above Design Flood Elevation and these functions and equipment should also be protected from wind forces, wind-borne debris and seismic effects. All critical equipment and interconnecting piping, wiring, and ducts should be elevated or protected as recommended.[6]

While guidelines of various agencies intend to build resilience to disparate hazards (earthquake and flooding in the preceding example), the safety requirements for the two kinds of hazards are aligned in opposite direction in the sense that where reduction of seismic risk requires the electrical components to be placed at lower elevations, flood risk to these installations may be exacerbated at these elevations. Hence, a threat-agnostic approach to incorporate resilience can neither yield the co-benefits for disparate hazards nor be ubiquitous across systems for certain hazards.

Case 2: "Fail-safe" versus "safe-fail" way of planning. One of the key design principles in risk management approaches is preservation of status quo, that is, avoiding the transformative change and minimizing the risk of failure. However, resilience approaches focus on adaptation to changing conditions without permanent loss of functions. Park et al. (2014) distinguish these two approaches by referring to them as "fail safe" and "safe fail". Let us understand this in the context of levees that are built for flood management. A levee is a man-made structure designed and constructed in accordance with *sound engineering practices* to contain, control, or divert the flow of water to reduce the risk from flooding for flows up to a certain amount. Historically, reinforcing or temporarily overbuilding levees for increased resistance against rising river stage has been one approach to manage flood risks to ensure that these remain "fail safe" in the event of design flooding. However, as the name *design flooding* suggests, levees are designed to safeguard the adjoining areas from flows up to a certain amount. However, this approach is inherently limited in its capacity to mitigate flood damage. On the contrary, Park et al. (2014) in their perspective article on resilience provided an example of "safe fail" being a typical aspect of resilience.[4] The Birds Point–New Madrid Floodway is a flood control component of the Mississippi River and Tributaries Project located on the west bank of the Mississippi River in southeast Missouri just below the confluence of the Ohio and Mississippi Rivers. Its purpose is to divert water from the Mississippi River during major flood events and lower the flood stages upstream, notably at Cairo, Illinois. This diversion is accomplished by inundating the floodways. In 2011, extreme precipitation on top of snowmelt led to intentional breaching of the levee at multiple places to (a) let floodwaters in at one location, and (b) to let floodwaters recede back into the Mississippi River. Artificial breaching of the levee represents an adaptation of infrastructure to manage the changing and unforeseeable conditions. This deliberate "safe-failing" of the structure minimized the adverse consequences of the 2011 floods and prevented a more devastating catastrophe.

Case 3: Bottom-up versus top-down approach. Risk and resilience paradigms can both work from components to systems (i.e., "bottom up") or from systems to components (i.e., "top down"). Conventional approaches employed by infrastructure engineers, managers, or policymakers have often tended to follow the bottom-up approach where, for example, the strength of beams and columns are examined first before investigating failure modes for an entire building or a bridge, after which investment strategies or policy decisions are made to local or regional scales (discussed in detail in Chapter 2).

Risk management strategies, when used in the context of these conventional approaches, have also inherited their bottom-up strategies. Thus, individual components such as structural elements within infrastructure systems have been designed to withstand known threats up to acceptable thresholds with the desire to prevent system failure. However, with increasing complexity and interdependency within and across infrastructure systems, bottom-up approaches may become non-optimal in terms of maintaining overall system functionality, and hence cost- and time-prohibitive exercises at best, or impractical and infeasible at worst. The resilience paradigm, first and foremost, attempts to preserve essential functionality and services at the system level. Thus, almost by definition, resilience approaches tend to be top down. Engineering design, operations, and maintenance may aspire to make a building or a bridge resilient, while urban planners and city governments may want to make an entire city resilient. Thus, the definition of a system can vary in terms of scale and complexity, but resilience is still attempted at system levels. These concepts may be illustrated through lifeline infrastructure networks such as Indian Railways or the U.S. National Airspace System (discussed in Chapter 4). A bottom-up approach could consider installation and facility management as well as the strength of structural components within an airport or in the context of railway stations and tracks. Risk management strategies may attempt to strengthen these components against natural hazards such as floods, earthquakes, or heat waves, or man-made hazards such as technological failures and even terror attacks. A top-down approach would attempt to maintain essential functionality, which could be defined as the ability to maintain pairwise connectivity (e.g., for a passenger or a freight to be transported from any one airport/railway station to any other airport/railway station). A resilience-centric approach would attempt to maintain as much of this connectivity as possible even under perturbation or stress, thus requiring a system-level optimization, which may then percolate down to the individual airports, stations, or tracks.

So far, our discussion to understand the difference between risk and resilience has been centered around infrastructures such as buildings, levees, and transportation systems. However, a comprehensive view of resilience needs to consider community and social issues including social connectedness (or community structures), policies, regulatory guidelines, and frameworks. A decision maker cannot implement systems and strategies that may be resilient if they go against regulatory constraints. Similarly, policymakers may not find it easy to go against stakeholder concern about near-term cost even if the longer-term benefit to multiple stakeholders may benefit from a new regulation. The situation often arises even in the best of governance systems, such as elected democracies where elected officials confront the challenge to balance short-term popular perceptions with longer-term needs of societies and future generations. Let us consider the following example:

Example 1.1

The city of Boston (in Massachusetts, USA) is trying to decide how to allocate funding to develop resilience to (a) a Sandy-like weather hazard and (b) a Boston Marathon–type terror attack. This is a short-term measure for the calendar year 2017 only, because a major overhaul is expected from 2018 onward. The total funding available to the mayor to enhance resilience for 2017 is $50 million. Latest intelligence reports indicate that the probability of a terror attack in 2017 is 0.6%, while climate scientists have calculated that the chances of a superstorm like Sandy hitting Boston in 2017 is 1.5%. The total expected damage from a Sandy-like event in 2017 is $6 billion, while the expected damage from a terror attack in 2017 is $4 billion. Let us assume that, per unit money spent to enhance resilience, the proportion of damage reduction is identical for the two types of events. However, let us also assume that the types of resilience measures for the two scenarios are different, and one does not help or hurt the other effort.

1. Based on the preceding information, what is the dollar value of the expected risk from each of the two events separately, and from both combined?

2. How should the mayor allocate the $50 million to enhance resilience for the two types of hazards, one natural and the other man-made? Is there a single answer, based on the information provided? What assumptions, stated or unstated, need to be validated to make even better decisions? Which of the assumptions appear viable to you and which appear problematic? Why?

Let us go through the various concepts introduced in this example step-by-step. First, we will compute the dollar value of expected risk from each of the two events, separately. Risk can be conceptually expressed with the following basic equation:

$$\text{Risk} = \text{Hazard} \times \text{Vulnerability} \times \text{Exposure} \qquad (1.1)$$

Hazard is often expressed as the probability of a threat, while vulnerability can be thought of as the probability of damage conditional on the threat. Exposure is the total value (e.g., dollar value) of economic assets and/or human lives that are subject to loss. In this sense, risk becomes a probability (in Equation 1.1, this would be the product of first two terms) applied to the total possible loss – in other words, risk can be thought as an expected loss. The first two terms in Equation 1.1 are sometimes grouped together to provide the probability of an event or a stress that can cause damage. For further discussions, refer to section 1.3.

1. Let us relate the current example to Equation 1.1. The hazards are (a) Sandy-like hurricane with probability of 1.5% ($p = 0.015$) and (b) Boston Marathon–like terror attack with probability of 0.6% ($p = 0.006$). The other information that is provided is expected damage given a threat. This

corresponds to the product of vulnerability and exposure (i.e., probability of damage given the threat times the total potential loss). The expected damages in the current example are $6 billion and $4 billion for (a) and (b), respectively. Thus, risk can be calculated as follows:

a.   Risk from Sandy-like hurricane: $0.015 \times 6 \times 10^9$ = $90 million

b.   Risk from Boston Marathon–like terror attack: $0.006 \times 4 \times 10^9$ = $24 million

c.   Combined risk in this case can be thought as the simultaneous occurrence of (a) and (b), and total risk thus associated would be $90 million + $24 million = $114 million.

Part 1 of this problem is quantitative and not open-ended. This part, as stated, can have only one set of solutions as expressed in (1a) through (1c) above. Engineering risks are often computed in this manner and then used for design, operation, and maintenance decisions. While some subjectivity may be involved (e.g., in design safety factors), the follow-on computations are based on quantitative engineering principles typically with closed-form analytical solutions. However, policy considerations can be a game changer in this context, as shown in part (2).

2.   Let us assume that the decision maker (in this context, the mayor) and the stakeholders who influence the decision maker (i.e., the electorate and the media) are all that may be described as rational actors. In such a situation, the allocation of available funds for minimizing risks may be based strictly on the quantitative computations. In that situation and given the assumption stated in the problem, the mayor would allocate $50 million in proportion to the risk posed by each event. Thus, the amount allocated to reduce the risk of a Sandy-like hurricane would be about $40 million (i.e., $\dfrac{\$90\ \text{million}}{\$114\ \text{million}} \times \$50\ \text{million} = \$39.48\ \text{million} \approx \$40$ million), and the remaining $10 million to reducing the risk of a terror event. However, policymakers can rarely make the rational actor assumption.

If the rational actor assumption cannot be assumed to be true, then a universally accepted solution may not exist. In fact, the problem becomes open-ended and potentially subject to human influences, such as the opinions and risk averseness of the policymakers and the stakeholders, among other considerations.

Just as an example, a mayor may be justified in thinking about public opinions and re-elections. Natural hazards are often viewed as "acts of God," and even preventable damages from these hazards are perceived to be beyond human control. Terror attacks, on the other hand, are by definition man-made, and hence human psychology can lead to the perception that reduction of terror risks may be a direct function of risk-reduction investments. However, irrespective of how accurate this perception may be, the influence on voters cannot be ignored. This may be exacerbated by pre-confirmation bias in situations where the voters may have a strong belief against the possibility of human influence on natural hazards. Under such circumstances, the mayor may have to take significant flak from the electorate for spending $40 million out of the $50 million that was originally available for reduction of risks due to natural hazards. This may be especially true if the electorate is not well educated about disasters and risk issues. In situations where the voters are indeed well educated, one could think of a reverse perception where excessive relative investment on the terror attack may cause a negative view of the mayor's decision. However, typically, even well-educated voters may find it difficult to get beyond the immediate psychological and emotional impacts of terror hazards. Thus, election may depend in a complex manner on the nature, extent, and intensity of the damage and the time between the event and the elections. Considering all these eventualities, the mayor may be tempted to allocate much more to reducing the risk of a terror event than may be justified by the quantitative computations alone.

1.2   Critical Infrastructures

Now that we have briefly introduced the concept of risk and resilience, let us get to the primary objective of this textbook: Critical Infrastructures (CI). Infrastructures span geographical and political scales (communities, cities, states, countries, continents, the globe), as well as sectors based on functionality (transportation, communications, energy, etc.). Thus, infrastructures may include buildings, bridges, and dams; railway tracks and roadways; airports, seaports, railway stations, and associated facilities; and urban, national, or regional communication, power distribution, transportation, and water distribution systems. In fact, in specific contexts, such as managing risks or embedding resilience, natural systems have also been included in a broader definition of infrastructures. Thus, levees along coastlines, designed to prevent floods from storm surge, may be further augmented by marine ecosystems such as oyster beds and mangroves, which in turn may reduce the magnitude of the surge. From that perspective, in certain cases, it may be useful to distinguish between natural and built infrastructures and, in some cases, consider nature-inspired infrastructures and the interdependent "system of systems" that results from the interaction of these natural, nature-inspired, and built systems. The rest of this section focuses on built infrastructures.

While all infrastructures may be considered critical depending on perspectives and context, the Department of Homeland Security (DHS), in the 2013 *Presidential Policy Directive 21 (PPD-21): Critical Infrastructure Security and Resilience*, defined 16 Critical Infrastructure (CI) sectors. These are defined as

> sectors whose assets, systems and networks, whether physical or virtual, are considered so vital to the United States that their incapacitation of destruction

would have a debilitating effect on security, national economic security, national public health or safety, or any other combination thereof.

These 16 sectors are Energy, Chemical, Dams, Defense Industrial Base, Emergency Services, Food and Agriculture, Transportation System, Water and Wastewater Systems, Communications, Commercial Facilities, Financial Services, Critical Manufacturing, Government Facilities, Health and Public Health, Information Technology, and Nuclear Reactors, Materials, and Waste.

Resilience can be defined across scales, which in turn dictates the scales at which the criticality of infrastructures need to be examined. Two common categorizations are (a) community resilience and (b) regional resilience. In the context of community resilience, the interaction of infrastructures at community scales (e.g., neighborhoods, villages, cities, counties) with the people and economic assets within these communities become important. Thus, the infrastructures of interest range from residential and commercial buildings, bridges, and emergency services. Furthermore, infrastructure sectors that may directly or indirectly impact the community need to be examined as well. Thus, the condition of levees, dams, and reservoirs may have direct or indirect impacts on flood hazards and water or food security. Similarly, the presence of a nuclear power plant in a close vicinity may impact the threat perceptions and hence needs to guide the preparedness, response, and recovery strategies. Regional resilience, on the other hand, is concerned with larger geographical scales and typically goes across jurisdictions, political (occasionally even international) boundaries, and multiple sectors.

The 2013 National Infrastructure Advisory Council (NIAC) report entitled *Strengthening Regional Resilience Through National, Regional, and Sector Partnerships* emphasizes what have been called four lifeline infrastructures and their interdependence (Figure 1.1). The executive summary of this report states:

> Strengthening the resilience of regions and their critical infrastructures is essential for achieving national resilience. Over the past decade, adjacent regions and infrastructures have become more interconnected, enabling local disasters to ripple across multiple jurisdictions and sectors, causing disruption and damage over large geographic areas. Resilience is especially important in the lifeline sectors—energy, communication, water, and transportation—because they underpin the most essential functions of business, government, and communities. Much has been done to build partnerships and improve resilience nationwide. But when disaster strikes, the biggest hit is felt by the regions and local communities that must respond and confront the immediate consequences.

Regional resilience needs to consider essential functionality or service levels at the appropriate scale. Thus, there is a need to ensure that resilience is, in a sense, *baked in* each of the four lifeline infrastructure systems, as well as the "system of systems" formed through their interdependence. The corresponding attributes of resilience are described in section 1.4.

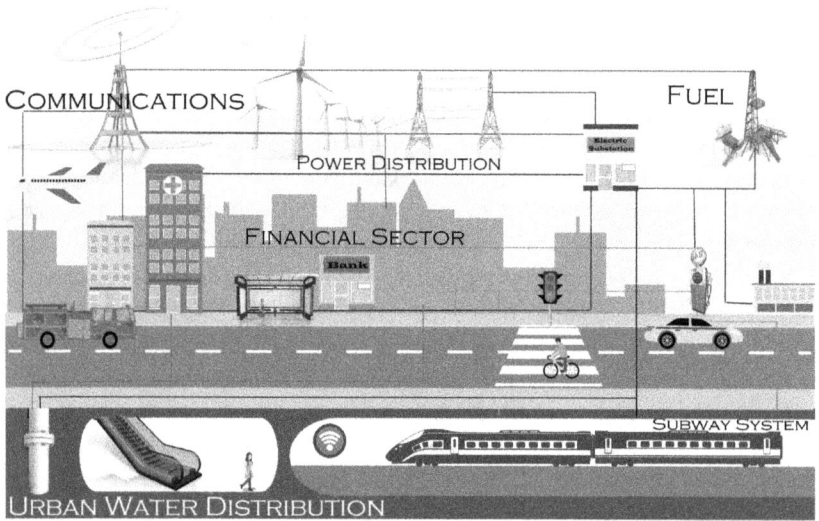

Figure 1.1. Interdependence among four lifelines in an urban setting. Four lifeline sectors—energy, water, transportation, and communications—are top priorities for strengthening resilience in all regions as they provide essential products and services that underpin the continued operation of nearly every sector.

Source: Partially inspired by Siemens Creating Resilient Cities.

Example 1.2

This example will take you through developing functional requirements in a way that can be communicated to policymakers. Consider the Massachusetts Port Authority (Massport) in the city of Boston, which is responsible for Boston's primary (Logan) airport as well as seaports and smaller airports in the region. Boston Logan Airport serves passengers across the Greater Boston region (population 4.7 million [2014 census, Metropolitan Statistical Area]; area 3,680 square kilometers [Metropolitan Area Planning Council]) and beyond. Following Example 1.1, consider the threat of a Sandy-like hurricane striking Boston and its impact on Logan Airport, including maintaining essential services during the hazard, and ensuring reliable, timely, and graceful recovery afterward.

(a) You have been employed by Massport to consult on facility-level risk and vulnerability analysis for the Sandy-like hurricane hitting Logan Airport. Perform a general literature review to understand basic facilities required for an airport to function and how they may be impacted by a hurricane in coastal cities. Once this is done, focus on the city of Boston and Logan Airport and find out as much information as possible from open sources. What specific infrastructures need to be protected from hurricane winds and storm surge (which may include floods due to the hurricane at high tide, and may combine riverine floods due to rain) within the airport facility, and what contingency plans should be made for their interdependence? Specifically, consider functions related to supply of fuel, communications within the airport, power supply, transportation across airport facilities, and availability of basic services such as water and food. Express the interdependencies through a diagram and discuss flood walls, placement of generators assuring communications despite power failure, and ensuring availability of resources. Prepare this diagram in a way such that major vulnerabilities, interdependencies, ripple effects, and risk management and mitigation strategies can be conveyed to Massport's upper management.

(b) Impressed by what you have achieved at Massport, the city and state planners of Greater Boston and Massachusetts have now employed you to understand the cascading effects of the hurricane's impact on regional infrastructure in Greater Boston with a view to characterizing the consequences for Logan Airport to function. For example, Boston's subway and commuter train system as well as bus and taxi services (including rideshare facilities such as Uber or Lyft) need to function for passengers to access the airport. The seaports and maritime facilities, as well as roads and bridges, need to function for the transport of fuel. The availability of basic services such as food, fuel, water, and sanitation also depends on transportation, communication, power, and the corresponding distribution and supply networks all working in tandem. Now for the Greater Boston area, but with a focus on functioning of Logan, repeat the exercise that you performed in part (a). In other words, discuss what lifeline infrastructure networks and systems may be impacted and how their interdependencies will play out in the context of preparedness, response, and recovery before, during, and after the hazards. Once again, express the interdependencies, vulnerabilities, and risk management and mitigation strategies through a set of diagrams. Consider the fact that unlike part (a), in this case, the need is to address multiple stakeholders (who may have complementary, supplementary, and occasionally even competing requirements) across jurisdictions, political boundaries, regulatory needs, and sectors. You need to convey to the planners and the policymakers how best to address the individual needs of the stakeholders while optimizing the service levels at the overall system levels, which in turn will ultimately benefit all stakeholders.

Probability theory is an integral part of risk assessment. Hence, we will discuss some of the basic concepts of probability theory that will be used throughout the book.

1.3   Primer on Probability and Statistics

Probability is defined as the likelihood that an event will occur. Probability measures the uncertainty associated with the outcomes of a random experiment. Probability is usually expressed as a ratio of the number of favorable outcomes to the number of possible outcomes.[1] Probability is always a number between 0 and 1. Mathematically, it is expressed as $0 \leq p(E) \leq 1$, where E is an event.

1.3.1   Associated Terminologies

Although the rules of probability are few and simple, they are incredibly powerful in application.

Let us illustrate the application of various terminologies associated with the theory of probability with an example of a coin toss:

1. **Random variable**: A variable quantity whose value depends on possible outcomes. As a function, a random variable is required to be measurable. The domain of a random variable is the set of possible outcomes. In the case of a coin toss, the domain is only two possible outcomes, namely, heads and tails. Possible values of random variables might represent the possible outcomes of a yet-to-be-performed experiment or the possible outcomes of a past experiment whose already existing value is uncertain. For example, in the context of a coin toss, X represents the random variable such that:

$$X(\omega) = 1, \text{ if } \omega = \text{heads} \qquad (1.2(a))$$
$$= 0, \text{ if } \omega = \text{tails} \qquad (1.2(b))$$

    Random variables can be discrete (e.g., a coin toss) or continuous (e.g., wind speed).

2. **Event**: An event is a set of outcomes of an experiment to which probability is assigned. In the coin toss experiment, potential events include occurrence of heads.

3. **Mutually exclusive events**: Two events are mutually exclusive if they cannot occur at the same time. In the coin toss, the occurrence of heads and tails in a single coin toss are mutually exclusive events.

4. **Independent/dependent events**: Two events are said to be independent if the probability that one event occurs in no way affects the probability of the other event occurring. For example, the probability of a coin landing

on tails is 1/2 or 0.5. The probabilities do not change on the second or subsequent coin tosses. This is because the events are independent. One event is not tied to a prior or future event. On the other hand, two events are dependent if the outcome or occurrence of the first affects the outcome or occurrence of the second so that the probability is changed.

For example, in card games, if a card is chosen at random from a standard deck of 52 cards without replacement, it will affect the outcome of a subsequent withdrawal. The concept of independent/dependent events is pivotal in risk assessment. For instance, the risk of many events is generally expressed as 1 event in every n years. This means that there is 1 in n chance of the given event occurring in each subsequent year irrespective of the fact that it has or has not occurred previously. The only time this probability changes is if the assumption on which the probability estimate was made changes.

1.3.2 Combining Probabilities

Let us consider that an example of a Sandy-like hurricane event is a 1 in 500-year return year event. If such events occur back-to-back in consequent years, the catastrophic impacts will be outrageous. Hence, risk managers and insurance industries are often interested in studying the combined probabilities of occurrences in the consecutive years.

Example 1.3

If the occurrence of Sandy-like hurricane events is independent, what is the probability that such an event will occur in 2 consecutive years?

Let E be the event that a Sandy-like hurricane occurs. Therefore, in a given year, the probability of the event occurring in any year, $p(E) = 1/500$. Because the events are independent, $p(E)$ in the second year = 1/500. Hence, the probability of the occurrence of E in 2 consecutive years is:

$$p\,(\text{Sandy-like event in 2 consecutive years})$$

$$= \frac{1}{500} \times \frac{1}{500} = \frac{1}{250000} = 4 \times 10^{-6}$$

Events like these are classic example of low-probability, high-impact events. When two probabilities are combined, rules of Boolean algebra are used. The two most commonly used Boolean terms are the logical "AND" and "OR." When two events are combined using AND logic, and in case of independent events, the probability of the occurrence of event A (hurricane in year 1) and event B (hurricane in year 2) is simply the product of two probabilities. Thus, probability can be used to develop an overall probability of the event. In set notation, $p(A$ and $B)$ is expressed as $p(A \cap B)$. Hence, for independent events:

$$p(A \cap B) = p(A) \times p(B) \qquad (1.3)$$

Often, we are interested in estimating the combined probabilities in cases when several events can occur, but any one of these events can lead to an outcome. We encountered such a situation in Example 1.1, where there is a likelihood of damage from both a man-made adversary and a natural hazard. For two independent events A and B, $p(A$ or $B)$ is equal to the sum of the individual probabilities. In set notation, $p(A$ or $B)$ is expressed as $p(A \cup B)$. For independent events, $p(A$ or $B)$ can be expressed as:

$$p(A \text{ or } B) = p(A) + P(B) - p(A)\,p(B) \qquad (1.4)$$

The two cases discussed before correspond to combining probabilities when events are independent. However, in many real-life situations, the assumption of independence may not hold true. For example, consider the combination of the first two terms in Equation 1.1.

As discussed earlier, in the probabilistic risk framework, Hazard (H) is expressed as likelihood of threat occurring, and vulnerability is probability of Damage (D) *given* that hazard has occurred.

We note that event D is no longer an independent event, but its occurrence is conditional on the occurrence of H. Combining probabilities of dependent events requires the understanding of conditional probability, which is discussed next.

Conditional probability is a probability whose sample space has been limited only by those outcomes that fulfill a certain condition. It is expressed as $p(A/B)$, which means the probability of occurrence of A given B has already happened. For dependent events, $p(A$ and $B)$ can be written as:

$$p(A \cap B) = p(A) \times p(B/A) \qquad (1.5)$$

For dependent events A and B, Equation 1.4 can be expressed as:

$$p(A \text{ or } B) = p(A) + p(B) - p(A)p(B/A)$$

Example 1.4 illustrates the application of conditional probability in the context of probabilistic assessment of hazards.

Example 1.4

In the context of weather extremes in an urban region, extreme precipitation events occurring on consecutive days often pose a great risk of urban flooding. For the city of New York, let us say that probability of flooding from a 100-year precipitation event occurring for 2 consecutive days is given by 0.6. Moreover, the probability of flooding from tidal surge independent of the extreme precipitation event is equal to 0.01. The probability of the occurrence of tidal surge on a given day is 0.3. What is the total probability of flooding on a given day?

Solution

Let F be an event that flooding will occur. Further, let $A1$ be the flooding because of 100-year precipitation extremes and $A2$ be the flooding because of tidal surge. Further, let p be the extreme precipitation event and T be the tidal surge.

Hence, total probability of flooding can be expressed as:

$$p(F) = p(E).p(A1/E) + p(T).p(A2/E)$$

where $p(E)$ is the probability of the extreme precipitation event, which in the present context is the 100-year precipitation event on 2 consecutive days. Mathematically, $p(E) = 0.01 \times 0.01 = 0.0001$.

Hence, $p(F) = 0.0001 \times 0.6 + 0.01 \times 0.3 = 0.003$.

1.3.3   Probability Distributions

The probability distribution of an event is a mathematical function that can be thought of as probability of occurrence of different possible outcomes in an experiment; for example, if the random variable X is used to denote the number of tails in the coin toss experiment. The probability distribution of X will take values of 0.5 for $X = 1$ and 0.5 for $X = 0$. Probability distributions are categorized as discrete distribution and continuous distribution.

An example of discrete distribution is a coin toss where the values of variable X are discrete. In the context of hazards and risk framework, common examples of discrete distributions are:

- The number of category 3 hurricanes striking the East Coast of the United States in a given year.

- The number of emergency calls from a given locality after an adverse event.

The alternative to discrete distribution is continuous distribution. An example of continuous distribution is duration (in minutes) of precipitation with intensity > 60 mm/hr. A continuous random variable can take a continuous range of values. Common types of continuous distributions used for risk assessment are:

*   Normal distribution

*   Uniform distribution

*   Chi-square distribution

*   Weibull distribution

*   Poisson distribution

*   Exponential distribution.

Continuous probability distributions possess a Probability Distribution Function (PDF). PDF is a function whose value at a given point in a sample space can be interpreted as a relative likelihood that the value of the random variable will be equal to that sample. The probability density of random variable X is usually donated by $f(X)$. However, for $f(X)$ to qualify as PDF, the area under the curve traced by $f(X)$ in its domain should be equal to 1. Furthermore, $f(X)$ should be non-negative throughout its domain. Here the relative likelihood is important in the sense that because a continuous random variable can theoretically take infinite possible values, the *absolute likelihood* for the continuous random variable is equal to zero. However, PDFs can help us understand the *relative likelihood* in the sense that 2 different samples can be used to infer the relative likelihood. Consider an example of an extreme precipitation event. In an equatorial city, past 100-year records suggest that a precipitation event of certain intensity can typically last for 2–3 hours on any given day. What is the probability that a precipitation event will last for 2.5 hours exactly? The answer is negligible. A lot of precipitation events will last for approximately 2.5 hours, but there is a negligible chance that a particular precipitation event lasts exactly for 2.5 hours. However, we can calculate the probability that the duration of event will fall between 2.50 hours and 2.51 hours by computing the probability of $(2.50 < X < 2.51)$, which in turn can be computed by measuring the difference in areas under the curve between two points. Finally, before we see the various concepts of probability in action, it is important to discuss the various terminologies that we will use throughout the book.

1. **Mean or expected value:** In probability, the expected value of a random variable X is long-term run average values of the repetition of the experiment. The expected value is also known as the mean, mean value, average, or first moment. Suppose that the random variable X can take values

a, b, or c with probabilities p_1, p_2, and p_3, respectively, then the expected value of X is given by:

$$E(X) = a \times p_1 + b \times p_2 + c \times p_3$$

2. **Variance and standard deviation:** The variance of a random variable X is the expected value of squared deviation from the mean, $E(X)$. The variance of X is expressed as:

$$Var(X) = E\left[\left(X - E(X)\right)^2\right]$$

3. **Probability mass function:** For a discrete distribution, the probability mass function is a function that gives the probability that a discrete random variable is exactly equal to a certain value.

While the detailed discussion about various distributions is beyond the scope of this book, we will discuss two distributions: normal distribution and exponential distribution. We will encounter these two distributions in many problems dealing with quantification of risk and resilience.

Normal distributions: Normal distributions (or Gaussian distributions) are one of the most popular continuous distributions. The normal distribution is a two-parameter distribution, characterized by mean (μ) and variance (σ^2). The probability distribution function of a normal distribution $N(\mu, \sigma^2)$ is:

$$f(x \mid \mu, \sigma^2) = \frac{1}{\sqrt{2\pi\sigma^2}} e^{-\frac{(x-\mu)^2}{\sigma^2}}$$

The probability distribution function of a normal distribution is shown in Figure 1.2. The normal distribution curve can be used to compute the relative probability. For example, the probability of X between 68 and 100 [$Pr(68 < X < 100)$] can be computed by the area under the curve between the two points (Figure 1.2).

Because computing the area under the curve without the help of programming tools is a non-trivial task, standard normal distribution tables are often used to compute the relative probability of variables. The standard normal distribution is a special case of a normal distribution with zero mean and unit variance ($\mu = 0$, $\sigma^2 = 1$). A normal distribution can be converted to standard normal distribution by using the following conversion:

$$z = \frac{X - \mu}{\sigma}$$

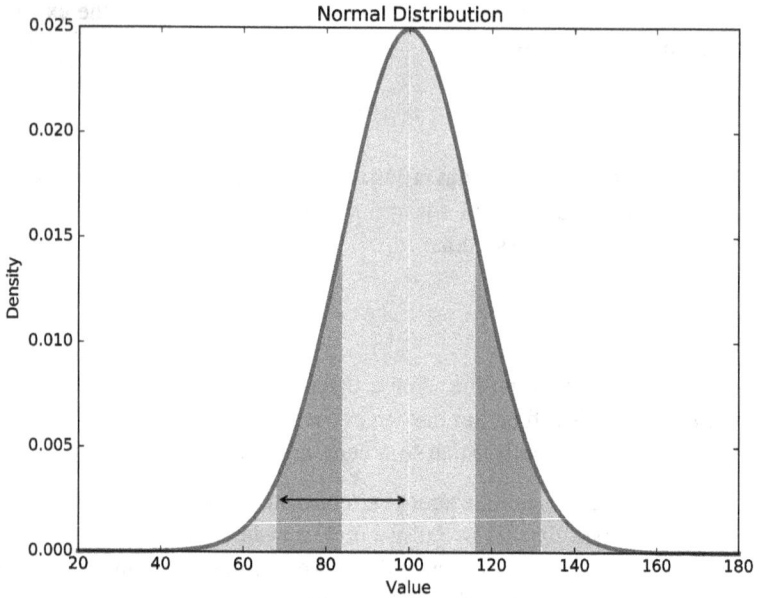

Figure 1.2. Normal distribution (or bell) curve. [Pr($a < X < b$)] is equal to the area under the curve between the points a and b, and can be computed using standard normal distribution tables.

Once, we have computed the z-scores for random variable X, we can determine the probability (specifically, the relative probability) using the standard normal distribution table (Appendix).

Exponential distribution: Another important continuous probability distribution for risk analysis and reliability engineering is the exponential distribution. The exponential distribution is considered to be memoryless (i.e., the outcome at the current time does not depend upon the outcome at a previous time step). Hence, these distributions are useful to model the hazards with a constant return rate. The expected value of the mean of a variable X that is exponentially distributed is given by:

$$E(X) = 1/\lambda$$

and the variance of X is:

$$Var(X) = 1/\lambda^2$$

where λ is the rate parameter (often expressed as per unit time).

The reliability of X at any time t is given by: Reliability(X) = $e^{(-\lambda t)}$

Example 1.5

Find the mean time to occurrence of a component that has a failure rate of 5 failures per year. Also, calculate its reliability for 5 hours, 10 hours, and 1,000 hours.

Solution

Mean failure rate, $E(X) = 1/5 = 0.2$ years. Here, the failure rate is 5 failures per year, or 0.00114 per hour. Hence, the reliability at any time t is:

$$\text{Reliability}(X) = e^{\{-0.00114t\}}$$

Therefore, for $t = 5$, 100, and 1,000 years, the reliabilities are 0.99, 0.89, and 0.32, respectively.

1.4   Risk Management Framework for Critical Infrastructures

In section 1.1, we briefly discussed the concept of risk assessment. In this section, we will introduce the risk management approach for critical infrastructure in more detail.

The potential for an unwanted outcome resulting from an event is determined by assessing both its likelihood and the associated consequences. Risk is influenced by the nature and magnitude of a threat, the vulnerabilities from the threat, and the consequences that could result. Approaches to understanding risk are likely to vary across sectors, industries, and organizations, depending on the operating environment and resources. Some of the risk assessment tools that are commonly used in the context of risk management are Preliminary Hazard Analysis (PHA); Failure Mode and Effect Analysis (FMEA); Failure Mode, Effects, and Criticality Analysis (FMCEA); event trees; Probabilistic Risk Assessment (PRA); and Critical Infrastructure Risk Management Framework (CIRMF), developed by the U.S. Department of Homeland Security to enable risk-informed decision-making related to the critical infrastructures. We will discuss CIRMF in more detail in the next section.

One of the commonalities across all these frameworks is that effectiveness of these frameworks depends upon analysis of potential direct and indirect consequences of an incident, known vulnerabilities to various potential threats or hazards, and general or specific threat information.

The Department of Homeland Security defines risk as:

> The potential for an unwanted outcome resulting from an incident, event, or occurrence, as determined by its likelihood and the associated consequences. It is influenced by the nature and magnitude of a threat or hazard, the vulnerabilities from that threat or hazard, and the consequences that could result. Risk information allows partners, from facility owners and operators to Federal agencies, to prioritize risk management efforts.[7]

Risk is influenced by the nature and magnitude of a threat or hazard, the vulnerabilities to the threat, and the consequences that could result, which is often expressed as the likelihood of exposure times the associated loss.

- **Threat:** A natural or man-made occurrence that has the potential to harm life, information, environment, and/or property. To quantify risk, the threat of an unintentional hazard is often estimated as the likelihood of occurrence of a hazard. Intentional hazards are estimated as the likelihood of an adversarial attack. Similarly, in the context of a nature hazard, threat is expressed as the probability of the occurrence of an extreme event (earthquake, hurricane, flooding, heat wave, etc.).

- **Vulnerabilities:** A physical feature or operational attribute that renders an entity open to exploitation or susceptible to a given threat or hazard. In calculating the risk, a common measure of vulnerability is the likelihood that the adverse event has resulted in damage given that the adverse event has occurred.

- **Exposure:** Reflects the level, duration, and nature of the loss resulting from the incident. Exposure is the total value (e.g., dollar value) of economic assets and/or human lives, which are subject to loss. In many risk frameworks, exposure and consequences are used interchangeably.

1.4.1 Department of Homeland Security Critical Infrastructures Risk Management Framework

The U.S. Department of Homeland Security recommends the division of identified risks into separate pieces that can be analyzed and evaluated individually. While developing the various hazard scenarios to identify potential risks for an assessment, various scenarios should cover the full scope of the assessment and provide the decision maker with comprehensive information. For complex systems, it is further recommended that critical components or nodes should be identified beforehand where security and resilience activities can be focused. The components of the Critical Infrastructure Risk Management Framework (CIRMF) comprise the following activities (Figure 1.3).

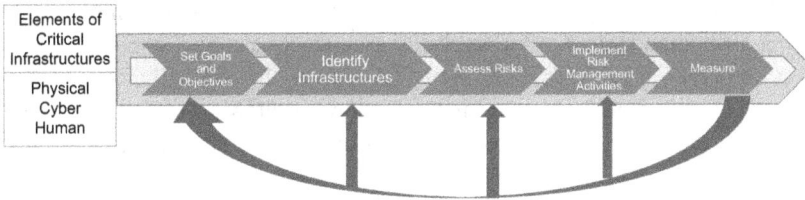

Figure 1.3. U.S. Department of Homeland Security's Critical Infrastructure Risk Management Approach.

1. **Setting goals and objectives** to define conditions, end points, or performance targets that collectively describe an effective and desired risk management posture. The overall goal of CI risk management is to enhance the state of security and resilience achieved through the implementation of focused risk management activities within and across sectors and levels of government.

2. **Identifying infrastructures, systems, and networks** that contribute to critical functionality and collect information appropriate to risk management including analysis of dependencies and interdependencies. DHS's National Critical Infrastructure Prioritization Program (NCIPP) identifies critical assets, systems, and networks as the entities, which if disrupted, could cause some combination of significant casualties, major economic losses, or widespread and long-term impacts to national wellbeing and governance capacity. The NCIPP identifies, collects, and prioritizes critical infrastructure information from states, critical infrastructure sectors, and other homeland security partners across the nation. It uses an enhanced infrastructure data collection application, which provides the ability to input data throughout the year.

Special emphasis has been laid on cyber infrastructure systems. The internet has been identified as a key resource, comprising the domestic and international assets within both communication and information technology sectors. The need for access to and reliance on communication technology is common to all critical infrastructure sectors.

3. **Assess and analyze risks**, taking into consideration potential consequences, both direct and indirect vulnerabilities to various hazards, and general or specific threat information. Threats and hazard assessments include various elements of both physical and cyber threats to critical infrastructure, depending on the attack type and nature. Hazard assessments draw on historical information and future predictions about natural hazards to assess the likelihood or frequency of various hazards. Hazard predictions also consider factors such as the impacts of aging infrastructure and climate change on overall security. We cover threats and hazards extensively in Chapter 3.

Vulnerability analysis identifies vulnerabilities associated with physical, cyber, or human factors. A vulnerability assessment can be a standalone process or part of a full risk assessment. It involves the evaluation of specific threats to the asset, system, or network under review to identify areas of weakness that could result in consequences of concern. Many Sector-Specific Plans (SSPs) describe different vulnerability assessment methodologies used in specific critical infrastructure sectors. The SSPs also may provide specific details regarding different ways the assessments can be carried out (e.g., by whom and how often).

Consequence and exposure analysis include direct as well as indirect losses and impacts related to public health and safety, economic losses, and psychological impacts.

4. **Implement Risk Management Activities**: Make decisions and implement risk management approaches to control, accept, transfer, or avoid risks. The results of critical infrastructure risk assessments inform the selection and implementation of mitigation activities and the establishment of risk management priorities for critical infrastructure owners and operators. The process of evaluating and selecting effective risk management activities generates information that can be used during incident response to help inform decisions regarding critical infrastructure restoration.

Risk management actions include measures designed to deter, disrupt, and prepare for threats and hazards; reduce vulnerability to an attack or other disaster; mitigate consequences; and enable timely, efficient response and restoration in a post-event situation, whether a terrorist attack, natural disaster, or other incident. The risk management approach focuses attention on those prevention, protection, mitigation, response, and recovery activities that bring the greatest return on investment, not simply the vulnerability reduction to be achieved. Security and resilience activities vary between sectors and jurisdictions and across a wide spectrum of actions designed to secure and strengthen the resilience of critical infrastructure. Risk management activities also may include the means for reducing the consequences of an attack or incident. These actions are focused on mitigation, response, and/or recovery. Often it is more cost-effective to build security and resilience into assets, systems, and networks than to retrofit them after initial development and deployment. Accordingly, critical infrastructure partners should consider how risk management, robustness, and appropriate physical and cyber security enhancements can be incorporated into the design and construction of new critical infrastructure and the redesign or repair of existing infrastructure. In situations where robustness and redundancies are key to managing critical infrastructure risk, it may be more effective and efficient to implement programs at the system level rather than at the individual asset level. For example, it may not be cost-effective to make every hospital in a metropolitan area resilient, but it would be prudent to make sure that geographically or otherwise affiliated hospitals are robust as a group or system, so that one can step in for another in the event of a disaster.

5.   **Measure effectiveness**: Use metrics and other evaluations to measure the effectiveness of efforts to secure the resilience of critical infrastructures.

Performance metrics allow partners to track progress against priorities and against their goals and objectives. The metrics provide a basis for the critical infrastructure community to establish accountability, document actual performance, promote effective management, and provide a feedback mechanism to inform decision-making. The national goals, which focus on risk management, shared situational awareness, and national preparedness, will be central to effectively assessing progress, providing a common understanding of the desired "end state" the voluntary partnership is collectively working to achieve. Developed through a participatory process involving a wide range of critical infrastructure partners, a complementary set of national priorities will illustrate the broad courses of action necessary to achieve the national goals.

1.5   Resilience Framework for Critical Infrastructures

Conventional risk management frameworks have focused on managing specific risks arising from hazards like an extreme event. However, with increased complexity and dependencies across critical infrastructure systems, all sectors (telecommunication, electric power distribution, transportation networks, etc.) are not well served by these strategies. For example, conventional risk management frameworks consider each hazard separately and often rely on historical data for assessment of loss. However, such frameworks may not suffice for unprecedented and/or unforeseeable hazards, and these events can result in catastrophic losses to critical infrastructure systems. With increasingly interconnected systems, which are vulnerable to threats brought on by sector interdependence, pandemic potential, and climate, all with the potential to trigger interrelated, cascading disturbances, it is important to consider resilience.

As noted in [1]:

> Resilience is not a specific, easily definable term. A myriad of definitions can be found in a wide range of literature, addressing all manner of public and private concerns. Some blur the lines between what is meant by critical infrastructure resilience, straying into the realm of infrastructure protection or community resilience. Though infrastructure protection and infrastructure resilience represent complementary elements of a comprehensive risk management strategy, the two concepts are distinct. Infrastructure protection is the ability to prevent or reduce the effect of an adverse event. Infrastructure resilience is the ability to reduce the magnitude, impact, or duration of a disruption. Resilience is the ability to absorb, adapt to, and/or rapidly recover from a potentially disruptive event.

Where:

- **Absorptive capacity** is the ability of the system to endure a disruption without significant deviation from normal operating performance. For example, fireproofing foam increases the capacity of a building system to absorb the shock of a fire.

- **Adaptive capacity** is the ability of the system to adapt to a shock to normal operating conditions. For example, the extra transformers that the U.S. electric power companies keep in store and share increases the ability of the grid to adapt quickly to regional power losses.

- **Recoverability** is the ability of the system to recover quickly—and at low cost—from potentially disruptive events.

1.6 Challenges in Quantifying Resilience

It is very difficult (and sometimes infeasible) to measure something without exactly knowing what we are measuring. The challenges associated with measuring resilience are broadly categorized as:

1. Conceptual challenges

2. Methodological challenges.

Conceptual challenges include:

- What are the decision boundaries (or thresholds) to classify infrastructure systems as resilient or non-resilient?

- What are the minimum levels of resources that are required to enable resilience in a given system?

- What are the geographic boundaries around the systems for which we want to quantify the resilience?

- What is the pre-existing adaptive capacity (ability to deal with change) of the systems? Adaptive capacity is the function of cultural, technical, financial, social, and political factors, and quantification of these factors is often elusive.

Finally, methodological challenges associated with the quantification of resilience are:

- Getting data that is reliable and meaningful, and capturing the evolving state of the system.

- Realistic modeling of the system for which resilience has to be quantified.

1.7   Exercises

Question 1: In 2005, Hurricane Katrina struck the East Coast of the United States and caused catastrophic damage. Similarly, in 2017, Hurricanes Harvey and Irma led to unprecedented destruction and evacuations in many cities. On the other hand, Amsterdam, the Netherlands, which sits seven feet below sea level, has been able to build resilience to destruction from raging storms. Compare the policies, practices, and perspectives in the two nations (the United States and the Netherlands), and comment on what lessons can be learned from the Netherlands to develop similar resilience practices across the United States to mitigate and adapt to such hazards.

Note

1   Naïve definition of probability.

References

[1] NIAC Critical Infrastructure Resilience: Final Report and Recommendations | Homeland Security; n.d. www.dhs.gov/publication/niac-critical-infrastructure-resilience-final-report (accessed August 29, 2017).

[2] Fisher, L. Disaster responses: More than 70 ways to show resilience. *Nature* 2015;518:35. https://doi.org/10.1038/518035a.

[3] https://emilms.fema.gov/is906/glossary.htm.

[4] Park, J., Seager, T. P., Rao, P.S.C., Convertino, M., Linkov, I. Integrating risk and resilience approaches to catastrophe management in engineering systems. *Risk Analysis* 2013;33:356–67. https://doi.org/10.1111/j.1539-6924.2012.01885.x.

[5] Linkov, I., Bridges, T., Creutzig, F., Decker, J., Fox-Lent, C., Kröger, W., et al. Changing the resilience paradigm. *Nature Climate Change* 2014;4:407–9. https://doi.org/10.1038/nclimate2227.

[6] https://www.wbdg.org/FFC/DHS/femap1019.pdf.

[7] https://www.dhs.gov/xlibrary/assets/dhs_risk_lexicon.pdf.

2 Probabilistic Risk Assessment

2.1 Introduction

Management of infrastructure systems deals with the systems that support human activities such as electric power, oil and gas, water and wastewater, communications, transportation, and collections of buildings that make up urban and rural communities. While infrastructure systems deliver essential services, provide shelter, and support social interactions, individual structures and buildings (communication towers, electric panels and sub-systems, pipelines, roads, etc.) essentially constitute the building blocks of critical and lifeline infrastructure systems. Design and maintenance of individual structural components or structures rely on traditional engineering practices, but in the context of infrastructures, system-wide planning emphasizes how different structures behave together as a system that serves a community's needs. Problems in this field typically involve a great deal of uncertainty, multiple and competing objectives, and sometimes numerous and conflicting challenges. The technical aspects of infrastructure engineering must be understood in the social, economic, political, and cultural context in which they exist, and must be considered over a long time horizon that includes not just design and construction, but also maintenance, operations, performance in natural disasters and other extreme events, and destruction. There are certain distinctions between infrastructures and structures that should be given due consideration while designing and managing these systems.

Structure is made up of several parts put together in a particular system; it can also refer to the way in which these components are arranged together. One of the most common examples of a structure that we encounter in our daily life is the building, where beams, columns, walls, slabs, and foundations are the constituent components. The aim of structural design is to achieve an acceptable probability that the constituent components and hence structures being designed will perform satisfactorily during their intended life. With an appropriate degree of safety, they should sustain all the loads and deformations of normal construction and use, and have adequate durability and resistance to the effects of misuse and fire. On the other hand, infrastructures are defined as the facilities, services, and installations needed for the functioning of a community or society, such as transportation and communications systems, water

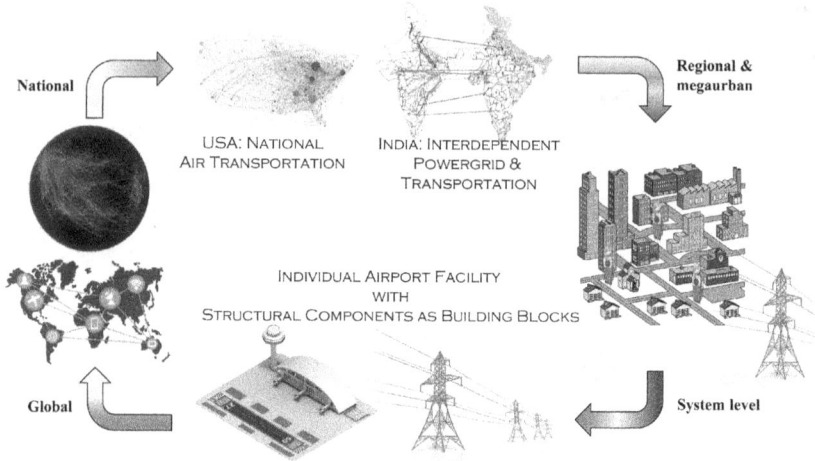

Figure 2.1. Enabling roadmap to efficient risk management and resilience strategies requires performance evaluation and risk evaluation of infrastructure systems operating at multiple scales. These systems range all the way from individual structures and facilities (e.g., airports, substations) to urban and regional systems (e.g., local transportation system that serve airports and help them maintain their indented functionality) to regional systems (e.g., national transportation systems such as the air transportation network of the United States, Indian Railways Network, and power distribution systems) to global networks (such as global air transportation and communication systems).

and power lines, and public institutions including schools, postal services, and hospitals. Infrastructure designing and management has a larger aspect, covering design, construction, operation, finances, and so forth. It generally involves a lot of stakeholders from various fields such as legal, financial, environmental, engineering, and governance and policy. Figure 2.1 shows the various scales at which infrastructures operate, ranging all the way from local to regional to global with individual components and structures as building blocks.

While high success has been achieved in applying the reliability-based methods for evaluating the performance of individual structural members, developing similar approaches for complex systems is still an active area of research. Evaluating the reliability of individual structural members is an important and indispensable step for evaluating entire structural and infrastructure systems. Identifying the relationship between the system and network performance to individual components is the first step in this direction.

This chapter lays the foundation for understanding conventional design practices that have been used for management and design and maintenance of structures and structural system. Critical gaps in current practices and proposed solutions are discussed in the context of both structures and infrastructures.

2.2   Risk Management for Structures and Constituting Components

Risks to systems arise from an inherent characteristic to make plans and try to make them happen, while external forces resist and tend to move our efforts away from the plan.[1] A system has a certain state in the present and subsequent states in the future. There are deterministic and probabilistic systems and corresponding approaches to analyze them, that is to make their current states apparent and predict their future behavior. Broadly speaking, in deterministic approaches, events are completely determined by a cause-and-effect chain, and effects of assumed causes are analyzed. On the other hand, probabilistic approaches reflect the consequences of failure, as well as the probability that failure would occur.

Traditional engineering approaches for risk management for structures and infrastructures have focused on deterministic methodologies (using a predetermined factor of safety for loads and materials, conservative demand and capacity assessment, etc.). Deterministic prescriptions on the system design can be characterized as predefined rules whose fulfillment provides sufficient confidence that safety goals are met. One of the underlying requirements is behavior of a system under examination can sufficiently well be described by compliance with these rules in a checklist format based on "yes" or "no" answers. The analysis results in determination of divergences of design and system states in the system compared with the requirement set in current regulations. The final result is "safe" or "not safe."

Because deterministic risk analysis is a point value calculation of the safety performance of a system into a space of all possibilities via a functional representation of the system, its main inputs are descriptive statements and conservative assumptions to guide against uncertainty.

For undertaking deterministic risk analysis, a number of "severity categories" for both likelihood and consequences of hazards are identified, and the severity category of each hazard is assessed. An example of such categories is shown in Table 2.1. In addition to a qualitative definition, a quantitative definition is generally added to ensure consistency in the course of the analysis and provide benchmarks. However, it is neither required nor mandatory to use these quantitative descriptions. The risk associated with a particular hazard is then composed of its severity category in both consequence and likelihood and is often expressed as a pair of characteristics. For example, from Table 2.1, risk represented as C2 will represent a hazard with a likelihood C (unlikely) with category 2 consequences (major). Deterministic risk approach yields a risk matrix whose cells express the likelihood/consequence category to which each individual hazard has been assigned. An example of a typical risk matrix scheme is shown in Figure 2.2.

The main strength of the deterministic approach is that the associated analysis and decision-making process is relatively simple and clear. The systems

Severity Category	Qualitative Definition	Occurrence Frequency (number of times/year)
A	Likely: once in a year	0.3–3
B	Possible but not likely	0.03–0.3
C	Unlikely	0.003–0.03
D	Very unlikely	0.0003–0.003
E	Remote	0.00003–0.0003

Consequence Category	Qualitative Definition	Occurrence Frequency (number of times/year)
1	Catastrophic	Multiple fatalities
2	Major	Single fatality
3	Very serious	Permanently disabling injury
4	Serious	Serious injury
5	Minor	Lost time injury

Table 2.1. Likelihood and consequence categories for deterministic risk analysis (From [1])

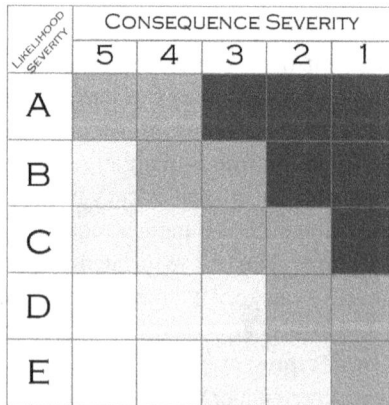

Figure 2.2. A typical risk matrix associated with deterministic risk approaches. Shade indicates the level of acceptable of risk. The darker the shade, the lower the acceptable risk. For example, for event A1, acceptable risk is negligible. That is, it is not expected that the system will reach consequence stage 1 under an event of magnitude A.

analysis and the associated calculations are straightforward, and the decision-making answer is "safe" or "not safe." It can be carried out with comparatively little effort and is suitable for use by personnel with a profound knowledge of the system design and operation, but not necessarily with an expertise in risk analysis.

However, a main problem with the deterministic risk analysis approach is that it relies on wealth of experience. Established practices are usually fine for dealing with high probability events where cause and effect can easily be demonstrated. In deterministic risk analysis, there is no explicit consideration of the various types of uncertainties, and there is a lack of consistent information about which criteria or analysis results are more or less important with respect to the overall safety level.

Trial-and-error risk management is unsuitable for low-probability, high-risk events. Examples of such events include tornado strikes, gas explosions, bomb explosions, fully developed building fires, and so forth. It is worth noting that frequencies of these hazards are not constant, and these can vary over space and time. Hence, the public perception of threat keeps changing. As a result, the performance of deterministic approaches mentioned above are not consistent with social objectives, expectations, and resources. Given the limitations associated with deterministic methods, Probabilistic Risk Assessment frameworks have been used extensively for risk assessment of systems and constituting components. Probabilistic approaches are covered next.

Exercise 2.1

Deterministic risk analysis often requires user judgment to assess the magnitude of risk categorization. Consider at least five hazards (e.g., flooding, earthquake, hurricane, tornado) of your choice and classify them using the deterministic risk classification scheme as shown in Table 2.1 and Figure 2.2.

2.2.1 Probabilistic Approaches

As discussed in Chapter 1, the basic ingredients of risk are probability of occurrence of hazard and consequences of the hazard (measured in terms of deaths, dollar values, or system downtime). Probabilistic Risk Assessment takes account these elements to answer the following questions:

1. What can go wrong with the studied technological entity or stressor, or what are the initiators or initiating events (undesirable starting events) that lead to adverse consequence(s)?

2.   What and how severe are the potential detriments or the adverse consequences that the technological entity may be eventually subjected to as
a result of the occurrence of the initiator?

3.   How likely to occur are these undesirable consequences, or what are their
probabilities or frequencies?

The probabilistic approach results in numbers, that is, probabilities of undesired
consequences, and can thus be used as an input to decision to system and constituting facilities safe. In a formal way, the instantaneous risk associated with
a certain event can be defined in the form of a risk density function (analogous
to probability density functions introduced in Chapter 1). The instantaneous risk
$R_i(\geq C_j, t')$ is the probability that an accident due to initiating event i will occur
at time t' and will produce a damage of consequence type j of magnitude $\geq C_j$
and is commonly expressed in form of risk curves:

$$R_i(\geq C_j, t') = \int_{C_j}^{\infty} R_i(c_j, t')\, dc_j \tag{2.1}$$

Where $R_i(C_j, t')$ is the probability density function resulting from an initiating
event i triggering damage of consequence type j of magnitude C_j (Figure 2.3).
Because $R_i(C_j, t')$ represents the probability density function, the total area under
$R_i(C_j, t')$ should be equal to 1.

That is, $\displaystyle\int_{-\infty}^{\infty} R_i(c_j, t')\, dc_j = 1$ (2.2)

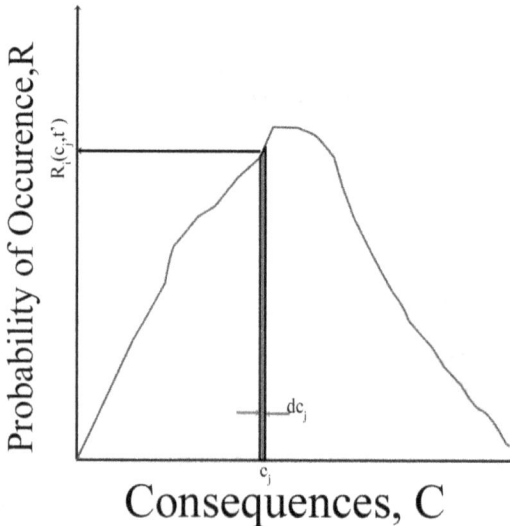

Figure 2.3. Risk in probabilistic terms.

Because the instantaneous risk described in Equation 2.1 is event specific, the probabilistic risk allows us to consistently compare the risks from several events. Moreover, event-specific risk densities can be summed together to develop the time-integrated composite risk from all accident initiating events.

Mathematically, the time-integrated composite risk for consequences of type j is:

$$R\left(\geq C_j, t\right) = \sum_{c_j \geq C_j} c_j \int_0^t R_i\left(c_j, t'\right) dt' = \sum_{c_j \geq C_j} c_j \phi_j\left(t\right) \qquad (2.3)$$

Where $\phi_j(t)$ is the time-dependent probability that the consequence of type j and magnitude equaling or exceeding magnitude C_j within the time interval t. To compute the values of $\phi_j(t)$, the frequency of event occurrence in a past observation time T can be used.

Example 2.1

The reinsurance company risQ Inc. has developed the risk profile for a city along the West Coast to compute the insurance premiums for major catastrophes. For a given year, probabilities of various events and the corresponding consequences in dollars are tabulated below. An event is considered to be a catastrophe if the loss resulting from an event is more than $100 million. Moreover, the probability of the occurrence of a forest wildfire within a year is time dependent and varies with the seasons. Summertime probability of wildfire occurrence is 1.5 times that of winter.

Event	Probability of Occurrence	Associated Loss (in million $)
Category I Forest wildfires (summer)	0.4	20
Category II Forest wildfires (summer)	0.02	90
Category III Forest wildfires (summer)	0.002	2,000
Flooding	0.002	4,000
Seismic hazards	0.005	6,500

Table 2.2. Deterministic risk classification scheme

(a) Compute the time-integrated risk for the city for magnitudes exceeding the catastrophic threshold.

(b) Compare the risks from forest fire–related events with risks from the other two events combined in a given year when thresholds are not accounted for.

Solution

(a) Using the formalism from Equation (2.3),

$$R(\geq C_j, t) = \sum_{c_j \geq C_j} c_j \phi_j(t)$$

Here, $C_j = \$ 40$ million. Hence, only category III forest wildfires will be considered for risk computations. Hence,

$$R(\geq C_j) = 0.002 \times 2000 + \frac{0.002}{1.5} \times 2000 + 0.002 \times 4000$$
$$+ 0.005 \times 6500 = \$47.1 \text{ million}$$

(b) Risks from forest fire–related events, say event i:

$$R_i = 0.002 \times 2000 + \frac{0.002}{1.5} \times 2000 + 0.4 \times 20 + \frac{0.4}{1.5} \times 20$$
$$+ 0.02 \times 90 + \frac{0.02}{1.5} \times 90 = \$23 \text{ million}$$

Risks from other events, say event j:

$$R_j = 0.002 \times 4000 + 0.005 \times 6500 = \$40.5 \text{ million}$$

Therefore, PRA allows the consistent cross-comparison of the risks from various hazards of which all have the same objective and is thus the preferred option in risk-related decision-making.

The application of PRA shown in Example 2.1 is generic and provides limited insights to stakeholders. In fact, when dealing with infrastructures and constituting facilities, stakeholders and decision makers often deal with complexities of the systems and uncertainties, both epistemic (statistical) and aleatoric (systematic), in determination of hazards. Conventional Probabilistic Risk Assessment methodologies for such systems conduct risk assessment for different external hazards by considering each hazard separately or independent of each other. The risk metric for a given hazard is assessed by the convolution of the hazard curves and fragility curves. The hazard curve expresses the probability of exceedance as a function of the intensity measure used to characterize the hazard. The fragility curve of an event is expressed in terms of the conditional probability of failure as a function of the intensity measure for a given hazard and is obtained by considering uncertainties in the available physical model. Mathematically, this convolution can be expressed as:

$$P_f = \int P_{(f|\lambda)} \cdot f(\lambda) d\lambda \tag{2.4}$$

Where $P_{(f|\lambda)}$ is the cumulative probability of failure given a hazard has happened. $P_{(f|\lambda)}$ in the context of structural systems is known as the fragility curve. $f(\lambda)$ represents the probability density function of the hazard curve. It is noted that obtaining the quantitative description of $P_{(f|\lambda)}$ and $f(\lambda)$ is a non-trivial task, and often requires well-conditioned empirical, experimental, and numerical simulation data.

A few examples of hazard curves that are commonly used for PRA of structural systems are seismic hazard curves, probabilistic wind hazard curves, flood hazard curves, and hurricane hazard curves. While discussion of the methodology to develop these curves are beyond the scope of this book, we can understand the application of these curves with the help of a few examples.

On the other hand, the fragility of system, structure, or component is defined as conditional probability to attain or exceed the specified performance function, Z. Mathematically,

$$P_{(f|\lambda)} = P(Z \leq 0) \tag{2.5}$$

Where Z is the function of random variables representing uncertainty arising from material properties, models, and external perturbations (loads or forces) acting on the system. In simplistic form, Z can be expressed as:

$$Z = S - R \tag{2.6}$$

where S represents the capacity corresponding to the specific condition and R is the demand corresponding to a given hazard intensity parameter. We will look at specific examples dealing with the solutions of Equations 2.5 and 2.6 in the context of structural reliability in the next section.

Fault Tree Diagrams

To quantify the total risk on a system or the probability of system failure, Fault Tree Diagrams (FTD) are often used. An FTD is a graphical decomposition of an event representing system failure into intermediate events through the use of logical expressions (such as AND and OR gates: see Example 2.2). Once an FTD is constructed, the next step is to identify minimal cut sets. A cut set is the unique combination of component failures that can cause the system failure. And a cut set is said to be minimal when, if any basic event is removed from the event, the remaining events collectively are no longer a cut set. A typical FTD, shown in Figure 2.4, represents structural system failure resulting

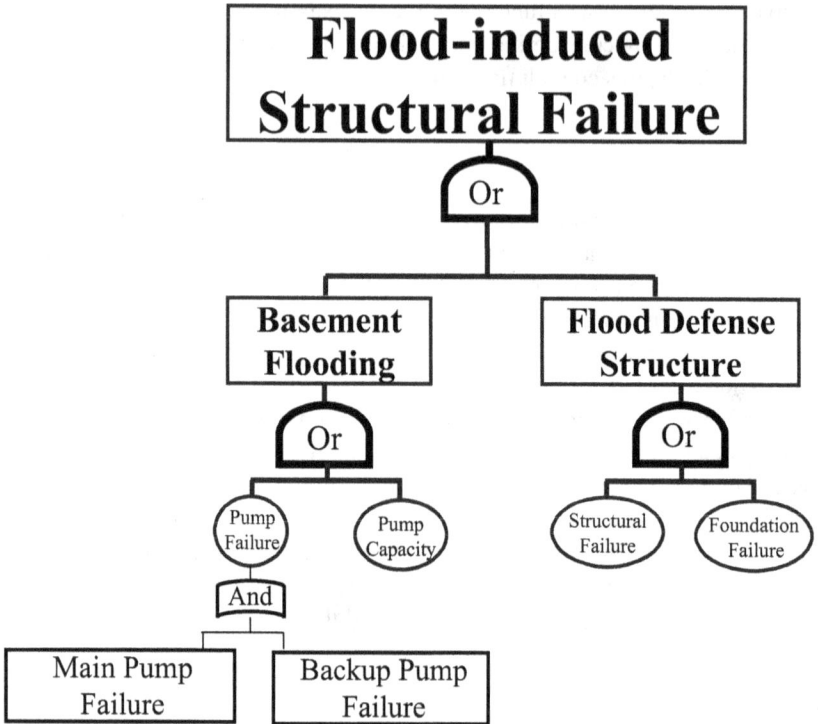

Figure 2.4. Fault Tree Diagram for flood-induced structural failure.

from flooding. Structural system failure from flooding can happen either from basement flooding or failure of flood defense structure failure.[2] Basement flooding, in turn, can happen because of pump failure or water seepage exceeding pump capacity into the basement. Similarly, a flood defense system can fail either because of structural failure or foundation failure. If we determine the failure risk associated with individual component failure, we can use the concepts of probability to compute the total risk associated with system failure (Example 2.2). In many examples presented in this book or elsewhere, you will notice that risk is just expressed in terms of annual failure rate or simply probability of failure. This is because certain failures in the chain of events may not have any direct cost implications, and hence it is difficult (and sometimes impossible) to associate monetary values associated with these risks.

Example 2.2

Consider the Fault Tree Diagram shown in Figure 2.4. The risk of failure associated with backup pump failure is 0.055, primary pump failure is 0.01, over pump capacity is 0.002, and structural failure and foundation failure are 0.004 and 0.0006, respectively. Assuming all failure modes to be mutually exclusive, compute the risk associated with flood-induced failure of the structure. [**Mutually exclusive**: two failure modes cannot occur simultaneously.]

Solution

To solve these types of problems, the first task is to identify all the modes of failures which can ultimately lead to the top event. The top event (TE) in this case is flood-induced failure of the structure. In the present example, this failure can be caused by the following three independent modes:

(a) **Pump failure:** resulting from the failure of both backup pump (C1) AND primary pump (C2)

(b) **Over pump capacity** (C3)

(c) **Failure of flood defense structure**: which can be caused by either structural (C4) OR foundation failure (C5).

Therefore, a total of four minimal cuts exist: C1.C2, C3, C4, C5 where (.) indicates joint occurrence of C1 and C2. The total risk associated with flood-induced failure (TE) is:

$$P(TE) = P(C1.C2) + P(C3) + P(C4) + P(C5)$$
$$P(TE) = 0.055 \times 0.01 + 0.002 + 0.004 + 0.006 = 0.00715$$

In addition to fault-tree analysis, Bayesian networks, cause-and-effect diagrams, and Markov methods are often used to perform comprehensive PRA on systems of varying complexity. Details of these methods are beyond the scope of this book and can be found in standard textbooks on risk assessment.

Now that we have developed the basic understanding of concepts of probability and applied these to a few simple real-world examples, it is time to introduce the concepts of probabilistic design and limit states in the context of structures. It is important to note that all modern building and bridge design codes are now based on limit states or load and resistance factor design (LFRD) concepts. Hence, before introducing the concepts of reliability, risk, and performance-based design concepts for structures and infrastructures, it is imperative to develop basic familiarity with the probabilistic aspects of limit state design.

2.3 Probability-Based Design of Structures: Limit State and Reliability Measures

Example 2.2 is an illustration of how simple Probabilistic Risk Assessment frameworks can be applied to model the failure of systems that comprise various heterogeneous components. As we noticed from Figure 2.4, failures of sub-components (i.e., failure of foundation, failure of structural components) trigger the sequential failure events ultimately resulting in failure of entire system. In this section, we will discuss the different levels of structural reliability methods. Subsequently, the concept of the failure function (see Equation 2.5) is introduced in more depth, and computation of the associated failure probability is discussed with the help of an example.

Failure of constituting components within a system generally refers to the event that make component(s) unfit to meet their functional requirement. Hence, in the context of structures, it is a fairly wide concept that comprises responses such as loss of stability, fractures, and excessive deformations. The consequences of various events also vary significantly. Collapse of a single sub-component does not necessarily imply the structure as a system immediately loses the ability to carry applied loads. At the other extreme, a sudden loss of stability is frequently accompanied by a complete and catastrophic collapse of structure. Failure can also consist of a complex sequence of unfortunate events, possibly due to juxtaposition of low-probability external or man-made actions. In engineering, distinction is typically made between different categories of design criteria. These are known as limit states. The three most common limit states are the limit states of serviceability, the ultimate limit state, and the fatigue limit state.

Reliability methods used in engineering design are generally classified as level I, level II, and level III reliability methods. In level I, the design procedures are usually based on point values for various design parameters and involve specific codified safety factors, which are intended to reflect inherent uncertainty associated with various parameters. At level II, information about variances and correlation properties in addition to mean values are also used for design. At level III, it is often assumed that the complete set of probabilistic information about hazard and structural response are available at disposal. Let us look at the reliability methods in more detail.

2.3.1 Probability of Failure Given Hazard

The common basis for the different levels of reliability methods is the introduction of a failure function which gives the mathematical definition of the failure terms. In order to estimate the failure probability, it is necessary to know the difference between maximum load a structural component is able to withstand, R, the loads it will be exposed to, and the associated load effects.[3] We already introduced the concept of failure function in Equation 2.5, and it is given by:

$$Z(R, S) = R - S \tag{2.7}$$

For positive values of Z, the component under consideration is safe. Hence, the associated region is termed as safe domain. When R is less than S, then the component is in failed condition. When the functional forms of R and S are known, we can formulate the probability of failure from a known hazard as:

$$P_F = \iint_{R \leq S} f_{R,S}(r,s) \, dr \, ds \qquad (2.8)$$

Where integration is performed over the failure domain, that is, the region where the strength is smaller than or equal to load effect. Equation 2.8 is known as a convolution integral, where $f_{R,S}(r, s)$ is the joint probability distribution of loading on the structural component and response of the structure. While close-form integration of Equation 2.8 exists for many of the standard distributions, computations of P_F for systems with multiple subcomponents often make reliability computations a known trivial task. Let us consider a sample calculation when forms of $f_{R,S}(r, s)$ are known.

2.3.2   Reliability Measures in Structures

As a special case, let us consider that both R and S are Gaussian random variables with known mean and variances (making it level III reliability analysis). Furthermore, two variables are assumed to be independent and hence independent.

Equation 2.7 can be used to write probability of failure as:

$$P_F = P(Z = R - S \leq 0) \qquad (2.9)$$

Now, if R and S are normally distributed variables, their sum (or difference) is also a normal variable. Hence, the mean and variance of Z can be expressed as:

$$\mu_z = \mu_R - \mu_S \qquad (2.10)$$

$$\sigma_z^2 = \sigma_R^2 + \sigma_S^2 \qquad (2.11)$$

Hence, the probability of failure in standard form can be expressed as:

$$P_F = \phi\left(\frac{0 - \mu_z}{\sigma_z}\right) = \phi(-\mu_z / \sigma_z) \qquad (2.12)$$

Where ϕ is the standard normal distribution function, corresponding to the mean of zero and variance of 1. $\left(\dfrac{\mu_z}{\sigma_z}\right)$ is known as the reliability index or safety index, and by defining the acceptable level of failure probability, one can find the corresponding value of reliability and vice-versa.

Example 2.3

A load-carrying horizontal member in a bridge is designed for a safety index of 2.5, whereas the similar member in a long deck bridge is designed for a safety index of 3. Assuming that both load and response variables follow normal distribution and are independent of each other, compute the reliability of the two components.

Solution

Here, β for two cases are specified as 3 and 3.5, respectively. All we have to do is compute the P_F. Further, because R and S follow the normal distribution, Z will also follow the normal distribution. Hence, solving $P_{F1} = \phi(-3)$ and $P_{F2} = \phi(-5)$ will give us the required reliability. Using the Standard Normal Distribution table (see Appendix), $P_{F1} = 0.5 - 0.4938 = 0.0062$ and $P_{F2} = 0.5 - 0.4997 = 0.0003$. Hence, the reliability of case 1 is $1 - 0.0062 = 0.9938$ (or 99.38%) and that for case 2 is $1 - 0.0003 = 0.9997$ (or 99.97%).

While probabilistic basis of design provides a systematic way to ensure safety and reliability of constituting components, Equation 2.8 on which this philosophy is based is not practical for analyzing or designing a realistic structure, even at a time when there have been significant advances in computational technologies. Samples of data used in reliability analysis are typically limited. For example, it is typical to have on the order of 25–50 years of data to describe annual extreme wind speeds or snow loads. Sample sizes of strength data (or structural response data) are also of the same order. Classical tests with the samples of this size may not identify the extremes of interest. Furthermore, the functions of R and Q represents the models of reality rather than reality. Failure probability estimates thus expressed in Equation 2.8 are subjective in nature and depend upon the choice of underlying distributions. Even assuming that models can be justified and calculations can be performed, there is still challenge in identification of an acceptable probability of failure for design and decision purposes. Finally, at the probability levels relevant for design (of the order 10^{-4}/year), Equation 2.8 is highly sensitive to the choice of underlying distributions. In fact, at these levels, equally plausible laws selected on the basis of limited data points can give rise to probability values which are several orders different in magnitude.

With the introduction of uncertainty measures to compute reliability index, the distribution sensitivity issue has reduced, and has led to a reduction of gap between models and reality. Most of the databases and tools necessary for development of first-order probability-based codes were in place by the late 1970s.

The LFRD specification for steel structures, AASHTO bridge codes, American Society of Civil Engineering standards, and many other codes worldwide have been offshoots of these developments. In the next section, we will discuss how reliability methods introduced in this section have informed the criteria for assessing the performance of structural systems and infrastructure networks.

2.4 Consideration of Risk in Component Design

Although the design methods that have been used in various codes and standards have accounted for design uncertainty rationally (e.g., reliability calculations discussed in Example 2.3), the outcomes of various natural disasters such as Hurricanes Sandy, Katrina, and Harvey in the United States and the 2017 South Asian floods were accompanied by major social and economic disruption. These events have highlighted that although prescriptive and quantitative design standards and codes are easy to enforce from a regulation standpoint, these codes are not sufficient to cope with the foreseeable yet unprecedented extremes. Hence, the role of engineering and designing should go beyond occupant safety to minimizing the likelihood of functional disruptions. This has led to the emergence of risk-based design for structural systems.

Risk analysis methods provide a means to consider the performance of the structural system including the probability of structural failure, P_F, and the resulting consequences. Equation 2.8 can be modified to give measure of risk as it is usually expressed, as the probability of failure (P_F) times the consequences of failure. The consequences of failure can be expressed in the terms of direct costs, such as the cost associated with post-hazard repair or replacement of structures; and indirect and user costs including social, economic, and environmental costs and downtime costs.

In the risk-based framework, the probability of loss for single or multiple hazards can be written as:[4]

$$P\,(\text{loss}) = \sum_H \sum_{LS} \sum_D P\,(\text{loss}\,|\,\text{Damage})\,P\,(\text{Damage}\,|\,LS)$$
$$P\,(LS\,|\,H)P\,(H) \qquad (2.13)$$

Where loss is the appropriate loss metric (could be direct or indirect loss), $P(H)$ is the probability of the occurrence of hazard (H); $P(LS|H)$ is the conditional probability of the component reaching the limit state of collapse given the hazard; $P(\text{Damage}|LS)$ is the conditional probability of occurrence of damage state given limit state has been reached; and $P(\text{loss}|\text{Damage})$ is the probability of loss given that the damage state has occurred.

Consideration of multiple hazards simultaneously in Equation 2.13 results in the elimination of potentially conflicting effects of certain features and hazard measure that could improve the performance under one hazard but aggravate the vulnerability to another hazard. An example of vulnerability aggravation is discussed in Chapter 1 in the context of earthquakes and floods.

To translate risk assessment into practice, risk-informed performance-based design (PBD) is gaining momentum in many nations. In PBD, the design process is aimed at meeting the performance expectations of the occupants and users. These expectations often exceed the minimum requirement established by codes, and in a resource-constrained setting, it may not be possible to meet all these expectations for each and every structure. Hence instead of a "one size fits all" strategy, performance-based codes make a distinction in the performance requirements for different building occupancy categories, depending upon the consequences of failure. PBD provides better interpretation than traditional perspective component-based methods for design and evaluation. It requires explicitly stated performance objectives for each hazard level, transforming these objectives to structural response requirements, and assessing whether the structure meets the stated objectives. While PBD has been in practice for design of nuclear plants, it has been proposed for seismic hazards, and other hazards are still under consideration.

Despite the advantages, risk-based design creates a new set of challenges. These challenges come in the fields of risk quantification and interpretation, system modeling, and risk communication.[5] Despite these challenges, there has been the intention across all design manuals and codes across the globe to converge on the use of member-oriented performance-based design methodologies.

For example, the American Society of Civil Engineers (ASCE) categorizes the structure based on risk to daily human life and the community. ASCE's Standard 7 classification system for natural hazard identifies the following categories:

1. Temporary buildings

2. Ordinary buildings

3. Large public assembly buildings

4. Essential facilities such as hospitals, emergency services buildings, and communication centers. The acceptable level of risk is related to the consequences and risk matrix analogous to Figure 2.2 has been developed. Performance objective and event probabilities for ASCE Standard 7 are shown in Figure 2.5.

Similarly, Australian standards also use a set of reliability indices ranging from 0 to 4.3 for a 50-year service period depending on the consequences of failure and the costs of failure prevention measures. The Canadian Highway Bridge Design Code recommends adjusting the target reliability index β_T values of bridge members depending on the failure mode, member behavior, system behavior, and member inspectability. There has long been a consensus that structural designs

LIKELIHOOD SEVERITY	CONSEQUENCE SEVERITY			
	CONTINUED OPERATION	IMPAIRED FUNCTIONS	LIFE SAFETY	INCIDENT COLLAPSE
SMALL 10¹/YEAR	ALL			
MEDIUM 10²/YEAR	II	I		
LARGE 10⁻³/YEAR	III	II	I	
VERY LARGE 10⁻⁴/YEAR	IV	III	II	I

Figure 2.5. Performance objectives and event probabilities as specified by ASCE Standard 7. For events with small likelihood, it is expected that all four categories of buildings will function. Similarly, for very large events, it is expected that buildings of category IV will continue operations; category II and above buildings are expected to perform to the standards to ensure life safety, and category I buildings are likely to collapse.

should aim to minimize risk by considering the probability of failures and their consequences. Yet, the routine design of structural systems based on formal risk assessment methods for all pertinent hazards remains a challenge because of (1) the difficulty of applying probabilistic analyses techniques when evaluating the performance of complex structural systems; (2) limited statistical data to model the intensities of extreme hazards and their effects on structural systems; (3) the lack of calibrated criteria that relate analysis results to physical structural damage; and (4) the difficulty of enumerating the consequences of failures and the allocation of quantifiable measures for these consequences. Ongoing research is making progress in resolving these challenges and is developing the necessary tools that will eventually facilitate the use of formal risk assessment methods on a regular basis. In the meantime, recent structural design codes and standards have introduced risk-informed performance-based design methods to support the application of varying target member reliability levels that depend on structure categories, modes of failure, and required levels of structural performance. This approach provides a transition between the traditional LRFD approach and a full-fledged risk analysis of the structural system.

2.5   From Structures to Infrastructures: Measuring Performances

Many events in the last decade—including cyber physical attacks, power failures extending into several days and over large regions, hurricanes, floods, earthquakes, and hurricanes—have exhibited detrimental effects on the infrastructure systems across the globe. Although member and component level approaches to measure reliability approaches are currently well established and have been the focus of discussions in this chapter so far, it is widely recognized that a component-oriented approach does not necessarily lead to an efficient utilization of limited resources when making decisions related to the management of existing structures or lifeline systems, especially those that may have been exposed to extreme events. For this reason, there has been growing interest in developing system-level performance design and evaluation processes. Specifically, system-level performance metrics and characteristics such as reliability, redundancy, robustness, and resilience continue to be defined.

The resilience of infrastructure systems is defined in terms of recovery, and functionality that must be maintained before, during, and after the hazards. However, given the resource-constrained setting in which real-life infrastructure systems operate, it is virtually impossible to have the same performance expectation from each infrastructure system. For example, consider the example of Hurricane Harvey, which resulted in unprecedented flooding in the U.S. state of Texas in August 2017. Such catastrophic and unprecedented events simultaneously impact almost all critical infrastructure systems in an area. Time becomes a critical resource during and after these events, and infrastructure systems that play a crucial role in saving lives (such as hospitals, water distribution systems) should maintain essential functionality at all times, and should regain their full functionality within days or hours[4] (Figure 2.6). Such systems, if resilient, will have the ability to reduce the chances of shock, to absorb the shock whenever it occurs, and recover quickly after the shock. In Chapter 1, we briefly introduced the concept of infrastructure resilience, and discussed why conventional risk management frameworks, although necessary, are not sufficient for complex systems. But embedding resilience into performance-based and risk-based design requires definition of clearly quantifiable metrics to evaluate performance as a function of time. There are numerous studies that have proposed the resilience index for several structural and infrastructure systems. Because most of the infrastructure systems, especially lifeline networks that include communications, transportation, energy, and water and wastewater, can be expressed in the form of networks, Chapter 4 covers network science–based performance and quantification in great detail.

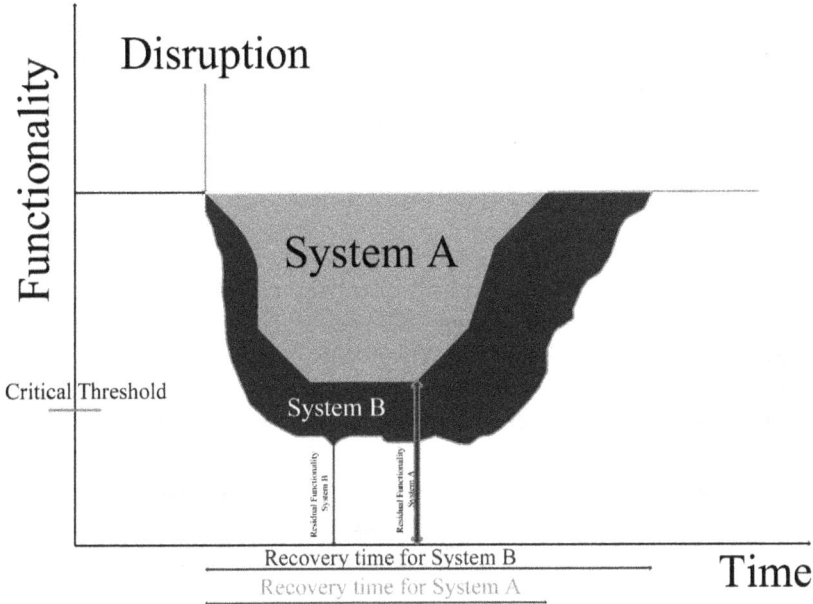

Figure 2.6. Resilience concept based on essential functionality and recovery time. System A is characterized by faster recovery time, and higher residual functionality before, during, and after the event is more resilient than system B.

2.6   Exercises

Question 1: The piping system in the system can fail either because of loss of coolant or because of loss of circulation. Loss of coolant can either be triggered by support failure of pipes ($C1$) or leakages of pipes ($C2$). On the other hand, loss of circulation can happen either because of excessive drift of the building ($C3$) or safety-related equipment failure ($C4$). The probability of failures associated with $C1$, $C2$, $C3$, and $C4$ are 0.0003, 0.000200, 0.000163, and 0.0007, respectively. Construct the fault tree of system risk. Also, compute the probability of failure of the system. [Hint: this example is adapted from [2]. Interested readers can read this paper to learn more about the Probabilistic Risk Assessment frameworks].

Question 2: You have been assigned the responsibility to provide consultancy for performance-based engineering (PBE) in upcoming mass transit system for a coastal megacity. The first step in the PBE is the determination of acceptable risks associated with events of different severities, and acceptable performance for each severity. This information is then encoded in the form of a risk matrix as shown in Figure 2.5. Design a similar matrix for the system. Clearly state the building types/services you considered within the system and the expected performance of each entity as a function of the severity of hazard.

2.7   Conclusion

Probabilistic Risk Assessment, which essentially computes losses based on hazards, vulnerability, and exposure, has been widely used across heterogeneous systems and diverse domains. The extent literature discusses theoretical challenges such as those arising from dependence among the three PRA elements, as well as practical considerations, such as relevance for early warning preparedness, communication, adaptation, and mitigation. In the context of infrastructures, PRA-based approaches have been widely used by structural and earthquake engineering communities among others. Recent advances include performance-based engineering. The concepts have been used for proactive design, retrofitting, and maintenance of existing structures and have been extended in recent years to critical infrastructures, including lifeline infrastructure networks. Recent developments in critical infrastructure resilience build upon, enhance, and encapsulate PRA-based concepts, models, and methods.

References

[1] Kirchsteiger, C. On the use of probabilistic and deterministic methods in risk analysis. *Journal of Loss Prevention in the Process Industries* 1999;12:399–419. https://doi.org/10.1016/S0950-4230(99)00012-1.

[2] Kwag, S., Gupta, A. Probabilistic risk assessment framework for structural systems under multiple hazards using Bayesian statistics. *Nuclear Engineering and Design* 2017;315:20–34. https://doi.org/10.1016/j.nucengdes.2017.02.009.

[3] Leira, B. J. Structural limit states and reliability measures. In: *Optimal Stochastic Control Schemes Within a Structural Reliability Framework*. New York: Springer; 2013, pp. 3–12. https://doi.org/10.1007/978-3-319-01405-0_2.

[4] Ghosn, M., Dueñas-Osorio, L., Frangopol, D.M., McAllister, T.P., Bocchini, P., Manuel, L., et al. Performance indicators for structural systems and infrastructure networks. *Journal of Structural Engineering* 2016;142:F4016003. https://doi.org/10.1061/(ASCE)ST.1943-541X.0001542.

[5] Ellingwood, B. R. Acceptable risk bases for design of structures. *Progress in Structural Engineering and Materials* 2001;3:170–9. https://doi.org/10.1002/pse.78.

3 Hazards and Threats

3.1 Introduction

Critical infrastructures are crucial to the health and welfare of the population and are especially important after extreme hazard events. If these facilities are perturbed partially or fully, the community cannot function effectively. This became painfully clear in many encounters with natural and man-made events in the past. For example, in 2005, Hurricane Katrina hit the Gulf Coast of the United States, which resulted in the overtopping of levees. The city of New Orleans and surrounding communities were uninhabitable after the hurricane. Damaged structures, in which people were trapped, were beyond the reach of fire departments because access roads and bridges were either flooded, blocked by debris, or damaged. Hospitals were unable to continue functioning or provide adequate care for patients. Communication and power distribution systems were brought to their knees, leaving large parts of the affected area without access to the outer world. The interconnectivity of our infrastructure can result in amplification of the potential of extreme events, and localized failure in one of the systems can propagate throughout the entire system, resulting in cascades of failures. Also, changes in various attributes of extreme events such as frequency and intensity, and changes in exposure as a result of urbanization, and migrations has made risk assessment of various infrastructure facilities a dynamic exercise. Reliable assessment of risk to such facilities critically depends upon the reliable estimates of hazards in addition to vulnerability and exposure. These estimates of hazards are often obtained by using mathematical models that represent various aspects of extreme events, such as location, occurrence, and size of events.

In this chapter, we will cover various aspects of hazard modeling. This chapter is organized into three sections. The first section deals with the definition and classification of hazards. In the second section, we will discuss the concept of hazard modeling, using floods and earthquakes as examples. Finally, we will discuss the evolution of hazards under global change and the strategies to manage risk under global change.

3.2   Hazards and Their Classification

A **hazard** is defined as a source of danger that may cause harm to an asset. This source can either be a property, a situation, or a state. It is not an event but a prerequisite for the occurrence of a hazardous event that may lead to harm to an asset. In other words, **hazards** have only a theoretical probability (or potential) of harm. An event that is caused by interaction with a hazard is called an **incident**. The likelihood of severity of the undesirable **consequences** of an incident associated with a hazard, combined with the probability of this occurring, constitute the associated **risk**.[1] Hence, hazards alone, in the absence of vulnerability or exposure, are just the potential to cause harm, but do not always result in risks. For example, consider a hypothetical snowstorm of the same intensity happening over (a) the continent of Antarctica and (b) the city of Boston. Although hazard is common in both cases (i.e., occurrence of snowstorm), the risk associated with events at both locations are significantly different. Unlike Antarctica, the city of Boston has built infrastructure systems, businesses, schools, and people who will all be potentially impacted by snow, wind, and cold. If a city is not prepared to cope up with the hazard, the vulnerability of exposed systems also increases, turning an incident into a **disaster**.

In the context of infrastructures, the 2013 *Presidential Policy Directive (PPD) on Critical Infrastructures* defines hazard as:

> a threat or an incident, natural or manmade, that warrants action to protect life, property, the environment, and public health or safety, and to minimize disruptions of government, social, or economic activities. It includes natural disasters, cyber incidents, industrial accidents, pandemics, acts of terrorism, sabotage, and destructive criminal activity targeting critical infrastructure.

Hazards can be classified in different ways. Based on the principal contributor to an accident scenario, hazards can be classified as:

- Technological hazards: equipment, structures, software glitches

- Natural hazards: precipitation extremes, heat waves, earthquakes, hurricanes, lightning, storms, high/low temperatures

- Organizational hazards: inadequate safety procedures, inadequate regulations

- Social hazards: hacking, terrorism, wars, arson, theft.

In addition to these criteria, hazards can also be classified on the basis of:

- Nature of potential harm: collapse, service delays, etc.

- Boundaries of the study object/system: exogenous and endogenous hazards.

Across the literature, the terms threat and hazard are often used interchangeably. However, the two terms have distinct meanings. A threat refers to the source and means of a particular type of attack that might exploit the vulnerability. For example, a flood (the hazard in this case) has potential to cause harm, but such an event becomes a hazard to us when it inundates urban areas. Similarly, a volcanic eruption is a hazard and resultant volcanic ash is a threat to air traffic crossing the affected area. Therefore, risk is the likelihood of being injured by the threat caused by the hazard.

The first question to be answered in the context of risk is, what can go wrong? Answering this question requires the identification of all hazards and threats and all the hazardous events that can cause hazards that can cause harm to one or more assets. Several methods have been developed for this purpose, and these methods are usually referred to as *hazard identification methods.* In the context of design and maintenance of infrastructures, the objectives of hazard identification are:[2]

- Identify all hazards and hazardous events that are relevant during the period of intended use and foreseeable misuse of the system.

- Describe the characteristics, and the form and quantity of each hazard: this is usually achieved by developing hazard curves that we discussed in Chapter 2.

- Identify when and where in the system the hazard is present.

- Identify under what conditions the hazard could lead to a disaster.

- Identify potential hazardous events that could be caused by the hazard or in combination with other hazards.

- Make operators and system owners aware of hazards.

The hazard identification methods that are generally used for infrastructure systems include:

- ***Checklist and brainstorming***: This involves developing a generic list of hazardous events and how these events may occur for the system being analyzed. For example, the U.S. state of Massachusetts has identified the hazards listed in Table 3.1 as relevant to the state. In addition to a generic listing, the state also defines the frequency, likely level, potential worst case, area of impact, and area of occurrence for various hazards.

- ***Change analysis***: Change analysis is used to identify hazards and threats related to planned expansion or modifications in the system during its operation. The analysis is carried out by comparing the system's state before and after the modification. For example, with increasing urbanization and

Natural	Man-Made
Atmospheric hazards	Bridge failure
Coastal hazards	Commodity shortage
Flooding	Cyber attack (data)
Fire events	Radiological device
Severe weather events	Transportation accident

Table 3.1. Generic classification of hazards

migration, coastal cities (e.g., Boston) and nations (e.g., Singapore) are expanding their urban areas through land reclamation. These reclaimed lands are often used to expand existing infrastructure facilities such as airport terminals, runways, and maintenance hangers. Such expansions on the reclaimed lands often gives rise to new hazards like flooding, soil liquefaction, and subsidence.

*   *Failure modes, effects, and criticality analysis*: The objective of this analysis is to identify all the potential modes of failure of the system components, identify the causes of these failure modes, and assess the effects that each failure mode has on the entire system. We already saw an example of failure mode and criticality analysis while performing Probabilistic Risk Assessment in Chapter 2.

*   *Structured what-if technique*: A structured what-if technique (SWIFT) is a systematic brainstorming session where a group of experts with detailed knowledge about the study object raise what-if questions to identify possible hazardous events, their causes, consequences, and existing barriers, and then suggest alternatives for risk reduction. SWIFT analysis often requires assessment of frequency and severity of all hazards.

In addition to some of the hazards that we have already discussed and listed in Table 3.1, some of the hazards can also trigger secondary hazards. For example, an earthquake can trigger tsunami, heavy rainfall can trigger landslides, and droughts can increase cases of wildfire.

3.3 Hazard Modeling

Needless to say, the mere classification and identification of hazards is not sufficient enough to understand their impacts. In order to comprehensively assess the potential of each hazard, one has to look at quantitative magnitudes of the potential and spatial scales of the hazard. While it is possible to assess the qualitative attributes of hazards based on the experiences in the past, an action-able prognosis often demands sophisticated modeling tools and methods.

In this section, we will look into these models in more detail using floods and earthquakes as examples. In case studies (covered in the next section), we will look at hazard mapping for both natural and man-made events with real-world examples.

3.3.1   Floods

The repeated occurrence of high-intensity flood events (e.g., India in 2016; Aus-tralia and Thailand in 2011; central Europe in 2013; India and Pakistan in 2014) has resulted in massive loss in the form of human and biodiversity losses, and damages to infrastructure systems. In the United States alone, approximately 75% of all disaster declarations are associated with flooding. Hazards associ-ated with floods can be divided into primary hazards and secondary hazards. Primary hazards occur due to direct contact with water, such as short-circuiting in electrical panels, loss of access due to submergence, and so forth. On the other hand, secondary effects include disruption of services in communication and transportation systems, and health impacts such as famines and epidemics, resulting in excessive demand on emergency medical services. Both primary and secondary effects are listed below.

Primary Effects of Floods on Infrastructures

- The high velocity of flood waters allows the water to carry more sediment as suspended load. This could result in damage and overtopping of levees and floodwalls, and collapse of buildings and structures that are in the way of the flow.

- When flooding recedes, the velocity is generally much lower and sediment is deposited. Everything is usually covered with a thick layer of stream-deposited mud, including buildings, roads, and bridges.

- Flood waters can result in massive erosion. Such erosion results in the undermining of bridges, levees, and buildings, resulting in their collapse.

Secondary Effects

Secondary effects occur because of the primary effects and relate to immediate and long-term changes that happen indirectly due to a flooding event. Secondary effects of a flood in infrastructure systems include:

a. Disruption of services:
- Drinking water supplies may become polluted, especially if sewage treatment plants are flooded. This may result in disease and other health effects, especially in underdeveloped countries.

- Gas and electrical services may be disrupted.
- Transportation systems may be disrupted, resulting in shortages of food and clean-up supplies. In underdeveloped countries, food shortages often lead to starvation.
- As a consequence of blockage of roads and bridges, emergency services, relief and rescue operations face severe delays in reaching the affected areas and populations.

Predicting River Flooding

Because floods can result in disastrous to catastrophic consequences for infrastructure, stakeholders dealing with risk, resilience, and insurance industries have great interest in developing flood hazard maps, so that mitigation and adaptation measures can be taken ahead of time. When water falls on the surface of earth, it has to go somewhere (it either runs off or infiltrates into the ground). The three main approaches used for flood prediction include (a) statistical studies to determine the probability and frequency of high discharges of streams that cause flooding; (b) using physics-based hydrological and hydraulic models to determine the extent of flooding possible when it occurs in the future; and (c) continuous monitoring of abnormally high discharges at measuring stations and gauges for short-term flood predictions.

Flood Frequency Analysis Both statistical and physics-based methods for flood forecasting critically depend on datasets and observations. Such data allows statistical analysis to determine how often a given discharge or stage of a river is expected. Rivers and streams are typically equipped with gauges to continuously monitor and record streamflows and discharge levels. From this analysis, a recurrence interval (such as 100-year and 500-year return levels) can be determined, and a probability of likelihood of a given discharge in the river can be computed for any year.[3]

- Data required to perform such analysis include a time series of yearly maximum discharges of a stream from one gauging station over a very long period of time.

- To determine the recurrence interval, the yearly discharge values are ranked, with rank $m = 1$ given to the maximum discharge over the years of record, $m = 2$ given to the second highest discharge, and so on. Thus, if there are n years of record, the smallest discharge will receive the rank of n.

- The number of years of record, n, and the rank for each peak discharge are then used to calculate the recurrence interval, R, using the **Weibull equation**.

$$R = (n + 1)/m \tag{3.1}$$

- A relationship is then obtained between recurrence interval and discharge. Using this relation, discharges corresponding to various return levels can be determined. For example, discharge corresponding to $R = 100$ years would be called a 100-year flood.

- The inverse of Equation 3.1 yields the annual exceedance probability, referred to as P_e. For example, a discharge equal to that of a 100-year flood would have an annual exceedance probability of $1/100 = 0.01$, or 1%. This would mean that in any given year, the probability that a flood with a discharge equal to or greater than that of a 100-year flood would be 0.01 or 1%. Mathematically, P_e is given by:

$$P_e = \frac{m}{n+1} \qquad (3.2)$$

- One important thing to note here is that despite the fact that the 100-year flood has only a 1% chance of occurring each year, the probabilities do accumulate over time. The probability of a certain-size flood occurring during any period can be calculated using the following equation:

$$P_t = 1 - (1 - P_e)^n \qquad (3.3)$$

Example 3.1

Using Equations 3.2 and 3.3, determine the probability of a 100-year flooding event in (a) 2 years, (b) 5 years, (c) 10 years, (d) 50 years, and (e) 100 years.

Solution

Here, the exceedance probability in a given year is equal to $1/100 = 0.01$. Hence, the probability of exceedance in n years is given by:

$$P_t = 1 - (1 - 0.01)^n$$

Therefore, $P_2 = 1 - (1 - 0.01)^2 = 0.019$, or 1.9%. All other calculations can be worked out in similar fashion. You will notice that the probability of exceedance of a 100-year flooding event in 100 years is not 100%, but it is around 63%. Why?

Flood Mapping Once the return level at a given station is determined, the next task in flood hazard modeling is mapping these hazards to determine areas susceptible to flooding when discharge of a stream exceeds the bank-full stage. Using historical data on river stages, the magnitude of discharges corresponding

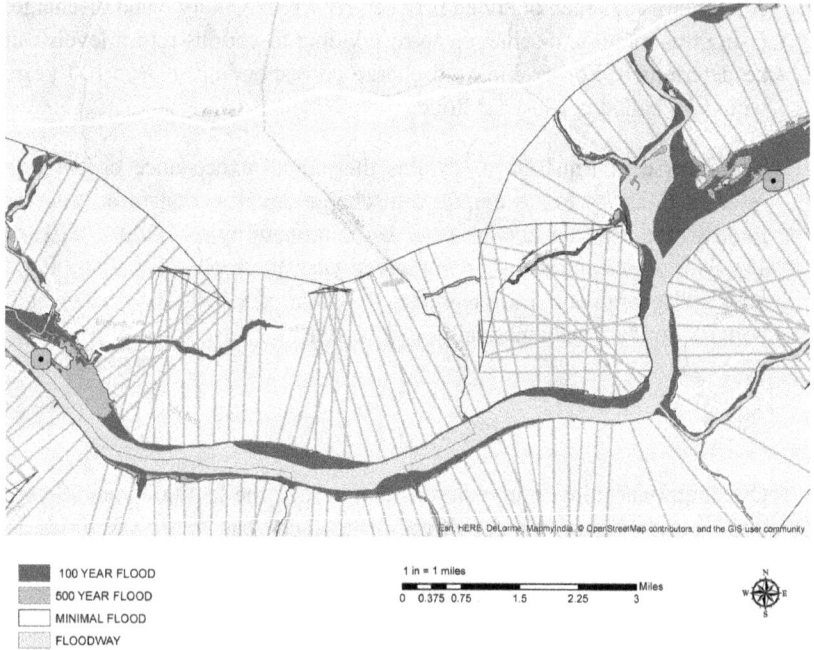

100 YEAR FLOOD
500 YEAR FLOOD
MINIMAL FLOOD
FLOODWAY

1 in = 1 miles

Miles
0   0.375 0.75   1.5   2.25   3

Figure 3.1. An example of a flood hazard map developed using HEC-HMS software. A flood map typically depicts 100-year and 500-year flood levels and protected floodways.

to various return levels are determined. This data is then used as forcing on hydraulic models, which use topographic data (to determine flow paths within and outside the channels if volume of water flows over banks), stream cross-sections (to determine carrying capacity of streams), and other relevant parameters (such as shape, roughness coefficient of stream) to construct the maps that are expected to be covered with floodwaters for various discharges or stages. Some common examples of hydraulic models that are used globally for flood mapping are HEC-RAS, HEC-GeoRAS, and MIC-SHE (Figure 3.1).

3.3.2 Seismic Hazards

In Chapter 2, we introduced the concept of hazard maps, which are used as inputs to Probabilistic Risk Assessment frameworks. The earthquake engineering community has pioneered the development of such curves and maps in the context of seismic hazards, and hence this community has lot to offer for learning in other scientific communities. In one of the editorial articles in *Science* magazine, the then editor in chief of the magazine wrote:

> The hurricane panelists frequently used the earthquake community as a role model to emulate. Annual events such as the "Great Shakeout" convince

people worldwide that they are vulnerable to seismic events, prepare them mentally to take action, and show them how to survive. Another promotion has been for residents in earthquake country to keep prepackaged earthquake survival kits handy. Both ideas are readily transferable to the many at risk from hurricanes. U.S. earthquake resilience benefited greatly from international collaboration with Japan, Chile, China, and other partners, who shared their knowledge of how engineered structures respond to various ground shaking, and their successes with early warning systems during rare seismic events. By comparison, hurricane resilience research has lacked an international perspective, despite the large number of nations that experience typhoons and similar severe coastal storms.[4]

In this subsection, we will dive into the basics of seismic hazard maps and try to answer the following questions:

• What are seismic hazard maps?

• How are seismic hazard maps used to inform infrastructure design and operations?

• How are seismic hazard maps read?

• Why and how are seismic hazard maps updated?

Seismic Hazard Maps

Seismic hazard maps depict the variability of ground shaking intensity during an earthquake. The map represents an estimate of the probability of exceedance of ground motion in a given time period. The hazard depends on the magnitude and locations of likely earthquakes, how often they occur, and the properties of the rocks and sediments that earthquake waves travel through. Earthquake hazard maps have been used globally to help establish construction requirements necessary to preserve public safety. A few applications of seismic hazard maps include:

• Development of building codes (e.g., ASCE 7, IS 800:2007, NEHRP)

• Highway bridge design

• Insurance and reinsurance industries

• Retrofitting priorities

• Allocation planning of assistance funds for education and preparedness

• Prioritizing retrofitting.

One important point to note here is that although there has been significant advancement in the area of seismic engineering for structures and buildings,

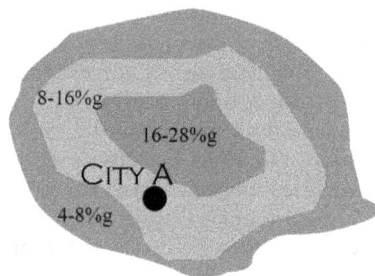

Figure 3.2. A typical earthquake hazard map showing variation of peak ground acceleration with distance.

seismic risk analysis for infrastructure systems is still an upcoming up and coming research field with multiple challenges and opportunities.

For a given probability of exceedance, seismic hazard maps are expressed in terms of peak ground acceleration (PGA) for a given probability of exceedance in a given time period. Peak ground acceleration is the maximum ground acceleration that occurred during an earthquake shaking at a given location, and is often expressed in terms of acceleration of gravity g, which has the value of 9 m/s^2 on average on the earth's surface. Hence, PGA of 8% g would mean that an earthquake would cause shaking resulting in peak ground acceleration of $0.08 \times 9.81 = 0.78$ m/s^2. Figure 3.2 shows a cartoon representation of a seismic hazard map (adapted from USGS) showing the distribution of peak ground acceleration for a region with probability of exceedance of 5% in a 50-year time period interval. For city A, peak ground acceleration that has a 5% chance of being exceeded in 50 years has a value between 8% and 16% g.

Probabilistic Ground Motion Maps

Probabilistic ground motion maps are contour maps representing the earthquake ground motions (of a particular frequency) that have a common given probability of being exceeded in a given time period (typically 50 years or 100 years). Probabilistic ground motion maps are generated using following pieces of information: (a) spatial location of past earthquakes that resulted in significant damage; (b) spatial location of past minor earthquakes to account for those sites where an earthquake is likely to occur in future; (c) historical maximum seismic intensities to estimate the hazard extent; (d) seismicity rates (frequency of past earthquakes) at different locations; and (e) model of future seismicity based on prehistoric geological information.

The ground motion coming from a particular magnitude and distance is assigned an annual probability equal to the annual probability of occurrence of the causative magnitude and distance. For large exceedance probability, the map will show the relatively likely ground motions, which are LOW ground motions, because small magnitude earthquakes are much more likely to occur than are large magnitude earthquakes. On the other hand, for a small exceedance probability, the map will emphasize the effect of less likely events: larger magnitude and/or closer distance events, producing overall large ground motions on the map. The maps have this format because they are designed to be useful in building codes, in which we assume that, for the most part, all buildings would be built to the same level of safety. For other applications, maps of another format might be more useful. For instance, many buildings across the United States are built more or less the same, regardless of earthquake hazard. If we knew that a particular type of building was likely to fail at a particular ground motion level, we could make a map showing contours of the likelihood of that ground motion value being exceeded due to earthquakes.

Example 3.2

The rate of earthquake occurrence in time is governed by a Poisson process, according to which probability of zero occurrences over a period of time is $e^{-\lambda t}$, where λ is the rate of occurrence per year and t is the time duration in years. For city of nowhere, we used the hazard map showing peak ground acceleration that has a 5% chance of being exceeded in 50 years. What is the annual probability of exceedance of such an earthquake?

Solution

Here, a probability of zero occurrence of earthquake in 50 years $= 1 - 0.05 = 0.95$, or $p(0) = 0.95$. That is, $p(0) = e^{-\lambda t} = 0.95$.
Taking the log of both sides:

$$50 \times \lambda = 0.05129$$

Hence, the annual exceedance probability or rate of occurrence per year $= 0.05129/50 = 1/974$.

Why Are There Different Probability Maps?

In Chapter 2 we introduced the concepts of performance-based engineering and risk-based design. These different probability maps are enabling inputs to quantify such frameworks. Given this design resistance, one might ask several questions:

- Under what ground motion will the building sway so much that it is uncomfortable to the persons working inside, and disrupts their work for the day? (This could occur with winds as well as with earthquakes.)

- Under what ground motion will the building bend so much that interior partitions crack and wall or ceiling fixtures drop?

- Under what ground motion will the building become permanently deformed and require expensive rehabilitation or abandonment? Under what ground motion will the building collapse during the shaking?

Hence, different probability maps are used to obtain performance of structures and components under different levels of hazards.

What Is a Hazard Curve, and How Is It Different from a Hazard Map?

While a hazard map shows the geographical distribution of ground motion for a given probability of exceedance in time period t, a hazard curve shows the probability of exceedance for various levels of PGA at given location. Figure 3.3(a) is an example of a hazard map for the entire United States showing distribution of PGA 5% probability of exceedance in 50 years, whereas Figure 3.3(b) is the hazard curve for a particular location. Development of a hazard curve is a non-trivial task as it entails models of future earthquakes, attenuation relations (i.e., how earthquake intensity decreases as the distance to the earthquake increases), and geologic site conditions. More details on how seismic hazard maps and seismic curves are developed can be found at the USGS website (https://earthquake.usgs.gov/hazards/learn/basics.php).

Recall our discussions from Chapter 2, where we used the hazard curves to compute risk to structures for various hazards. The risk metric for a given hazard is assessed by the convolution of the hazard curves and fragility curves. The hazard curve expresses the probability of exceedance as a function of the intensity measure used to characterize the hazard. The fragility curve of an event is expressed in terms of conditional probability of failure as a function of the intensity measure for a given hazard and is obtained by considering uncertainties in the available physical model. Mathematically, this convolution can be expressed as:

$$P_f = \int P_{(f|\lambda)} \cdot f(\lambda) d\lambda \tag{3.4}$$

Where $P_{(f|\lambda)}$ is cumulative probability of failure given hazard has happened. $P_{(f|\lambda)}$ in the context of structural systems is known as a fragility curve. $f(\lambda)$ represents the probability density function of the **hazard curve**.

(b)

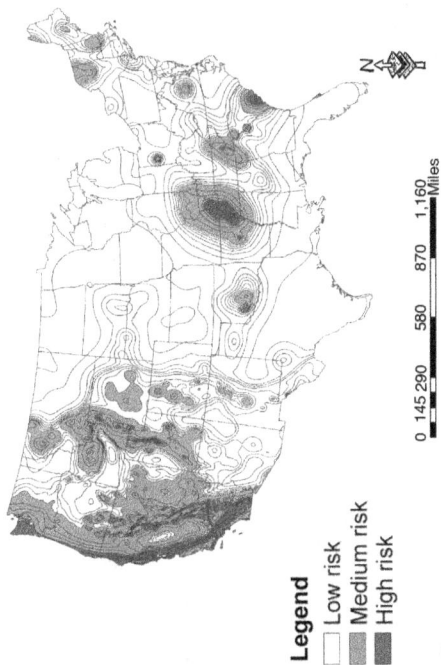

Ground motion likely to be exceeded every year

Design of buildings, schools, and hospitals

Design of nuclear power plant

Peak Ground Acceleration

1 in 1 years

1 in 500 years

1 in 10,000 years

Annual Probability of Exceedence

(a)

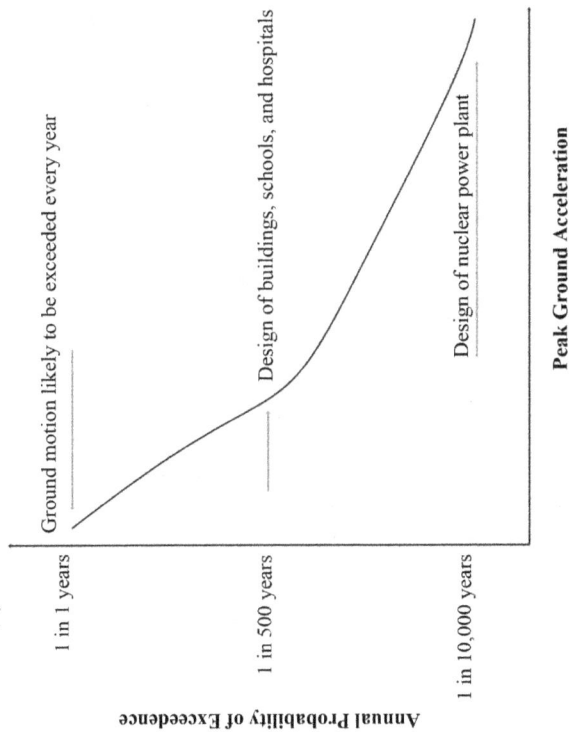

Legend

☐ Low risk
▨ Medium risk
▧ High risk

N

0 145 290   580   870   1,160
                                    Miles

Figure 3.3. (a) Hazard map for the United States showing distribution of seismic risk at 5% probability of exceedance in 50 years; (b) hazard curve for a location showing annual probability of exceedance as a function of peak ground acceleration

Exercise 3.1

Now that you are familiar with the technique of hazard modeling, discuss the hazard modeling technique for your choice of hazard. Your analysis should answer the following questions:

a.   What are the primary and secondary impacts on structures and infrastructural systems?

b.   Which type of method(s) is used to model the hazard (statistical, physics-based, or hybrid)?

c.   What are the data inputs of the hazard model?

d.   How are hazard maps and curves expressed? What values/parameters are plotted on the hazard map?

3.4   Concurrent and Correlated Hazards

All the examples that we have discussed so far correspond to single and independent hazards. A single hazard, such as Hurricane Katrina, the 9/11 terror attacks in the United States, or the 2005 Mumbai floods, may have debilitating short-term effects on human lives and property as well as long-lasting effects on economic growth and sustainability. City planners, policymakers, security managers, and insurance companies care about managing and mitigating such hazards. However, resource managers, multinational companies, and reinsurance companies (reinsurers insure the insurers) are at least as worried, if not more, about "correlated" or "compound" hazards. Correlation in this context is used loosely (as opposed to rigorous statistical definitions) to indicate co-occurrence of supplementary, complementary, or independent events. The correlation in this case may refer to events that are simultaneous in time and co-located in space as well as events that are either dependent or have cumulative effects but are separated in space and time. Let us consider an example of urban floods.

Example 3.3

Urban areas have a large fraction of paved surfaces, which reduces the amount of water that can infiltrate into the soil or be absorbed by vegetation. Thus, the relation between extreme precipitation and extreme floods are usually more direct. Let us consider a hypothetical example where a 100-year precipitation event always causes a 100-year flood event, and this 100-year flood event can only be caused by the 100-year precipitation event. What is the probability of simultaneous occurrence of the two events?

In this case, given the assumption of an exact (causal) relationship, the simultaneous occurrence remains a 100-year event (or in other words, the chances of those two events occurring in any given year remains 1/100 or 1%).

Example 3.4

Now consider a completely different example: two near-simultaneous events in the last week of August of 2017: (a) the flooding of Mumbai, India, resulting from extreme monsoonal precipitation, and (b) the flooding of Houston from Hurricane Harvey (which has been called a 500-year event). A seemingly reasonable assumption would be that these two events, separated by about 9,000 miles and caused by different meteorological drivers, were completely independent of each other. By the way (to our knowledge), while no specific and credible assessments exist for a return period for large Mumbai floods (such as the flood events of 2005 and 2017), let us assume for the sake of this problem that the 2017 Mumbai flood was a 200-year event. Multinational businesses and reinsurance companies may need to understand the possibility of the joint occurrence of such events, even under the assumption that they are completely independent. The question is, how do we calculate this joint probability under the assumptions?

Here, the probability of occurrence of flooding in Houston, $p(A) = 1/500$; the probability of occurrence of flooding in Mumbai, $p(B) = 1/200$. As the two events are independent, their joint probability is simply the product of the probability of occurrence of individual events. Therefore, $p(A \text{ and } B) = p(A) \times p(B) = 1/500 \times 1/200 = 1/10,000$ or 0.001%. In other words, such an event is a 1 in 10,000-year event.

Now let us extend this example and consider the following assumption: the two flooding events are correlated. While this may appear unrealistic at first glance, this is not as improbable as it may sound. First, certain climate scientists have hypothesized that global warming may intensify rainfall extremes resulting from the Indian monsoons. Second, other scientists have suggested that atmospheric and oceanic warming, caused in turn by global warming, may intensify rainfall extremes generated from hurricanes in the United States. While no scientists would ascribe global warming as the only cause for the intensification of the rainfall extremes under these two circumstances, the influence of global warming on each of these events may cause them to display some degree of correlation. While these correlations may be difficult to compute just from observations, or even from most typical model simulations, insurance companies and risk modelers sometimes do generate thousands and even hundreds of thousands of probabilistic simulations to understand these kinds of risks. Let us consider a situation where one million such probabilistic runs, carefully designed to consider the full spectrum of possibilities, are examined to count the number of runs where both these extreme events were simulated. One question is, assuming the independence assumptions stated previously, what would be the approximate number of runs (out of the million) where we would expect to have these two extreme events co-occur? As we calculated previously, the simultaneous occurrence would be a 10,000-year event. Hence, the expected number of runs showing this co-occurrence would be 1 million divided by 10,000, or 100. However, if such runs are statistically significantly different from 100, then we would begin to question some of the underlying assumptions. Thus, if the number of runs showing this co-occurrence were to be 100,000, this may indicate the level of dependence (potentially caused by the impacts of global warming or even natural climate variability other factors on both these events) is significant, even more than most climate scientists would suggest at this time. Computation of dependence among extremes may get fairly involved statistically and may require an understanding of the causal drivers. Thus, best practices in risk modeling often do have to rely on numerical simulations almost exclusively.

"Correlation" in the risk and hazard industry, and even in the research literature, is an overloaded term that may mean different things to different people. Statistically speaking, correlation is just a measure of co-occurrence, and as scientists, engineers, and statisticians love to say: "correlation does not necessarily imply causality." However, correlation may indeed be an indication of causality, either directly (such as the preceding floods and precipitation example), or indirectly (e.g., a third variable influences two correlated variables, such as global warming potentially influencing rainfall extremes and hence floods in Houston and Mumbai in the previous example). Compound events, on the other hand, may refer to a set of co-occurring events which together cause an extreme. Thus, in coastal cities around the world, extreme floods around the world may result from the simultaneous occurrence of heavy precipitation–induced riverine flooding together with tidal surge (which in turn may be exacerbated by coastal storms). This is often true in Mumbai, for example, during the damage in the 2005 floods. The co-occurring events do not necessarily need to be exactly simultaneous to produce extreme impacts. Thus, large floods in the Mississippi River basin in the United States are often caused by the time history of the rainfall and corresponding antecedent soil moisture, rather than from one heavy precipitation event. Similarly, an earthquake in California or in the Pacific Northwest, followed by a tsunami, would potentially cause more damage than either of these events alone.

One other example is when city planners or port authorities in Boston may need to consider the damage from a massive snowstorm in the winter (such as the 2013 winter storm Nemo) caused after damage from Sandy-like hurricanes in the fall.

"Correlations" in the world of hazards risk modeling may also loosely characterize the relation among natural and human causes as well as impacts and vulnerability related to hazards. For example, the massive earthquake in Taiwan (a global semiconductor manufacturing hub) on September 21, 1999, not only resulted in loss of lives and assets, but it also sent shock waves through the global semiconductor industry. To quote a report in the *New York Times*, the aftereffects "could delay or reduce the production of high-technology items ranging from cellular phones to Furby dolls—affecting far more than just the computer semiconductors that Taiwan manufactures in large quantities."[5] Another case in point is the devastating Thailand floods of 2011. In fact, interannual rainfall variability led to droughts in 2010 but floods in 2011. In terms of causality, there have been anecdotal verbal reports that experiences from a previous drought event caused human decision makers to operate hydraulic infrastructures (such as dams and reservoirs) in ways that magnified the flood event. From an impact perspective, because a majority of computer hard drives were manufactured in Thailand, the price of computers jumped up across the world, including in the United States. In fact, not only was a worldwide falling trend in hard disk prices reversed but an increase of about 40% resulted almost immediately, which took a couple of years to subside.

3.5 Evolution of Risks Under Global Change

In Chapters 2 and 3, we discussed a few examples regarding how conventional risk assessment and hazard mapping frameworks are used to make engineering decisions. One of the implicit assumptions that is often made in these frameworks is that the underlying probability distributions of hazard, vulnerability, and exposure are assumed to be stationary, and hence historical data can be used as a "guiding light" for the future. However, there is evidence that attributes of certain extremes (such as intensity, duration, and frequency) have changed as a result of anthropogenic influences, including increases in atmospheric concentrations of greenhouse gases. Settlement patterns, urbanization, and changes in socioeconomic conditions have all influenced observed trends in exposure and vulnerability to extremes. Rapid urbanization and the growth of megacities, especially in developing countries, have led to the emergence of highly vulnerable urban communities, particularly through informal settlements and inadequate land management. There is evidence from observations gathered since 1950 of change in some extremes. Confidence in observed changes in extremes depends on the quality and quantity of data and the availability of studies analyzing these data, which vary across regions and for different extremes. Therefore, given enough evidence of change in the past century, it is crucial to account for these changes in the present-day risk management frameworks to inform adaptation strategies in changing climate. The first step toward informing these adaptation strategies is the identification of drivers of change in present risk (which includes identification of changes in attributes of hazards, vulnerability, and exposure).

3.5.1   Changes in Weather and Climate Extremes

To quantify changes in attributes of weather and climate extremes (e.g., precipitation, heat waves, droughts), weather models (e.g., Weather Research and Forecasting model, or WRF) and general circulation models (GCMs) have been used extensively by researchers and agencies. These models represent the physical processes in the atmosphere, oceans, land surfaces, and cryosphere, and are the most advanced tools to date to simulate the response of the global climate system to increased concentrations of greenhouse gases. GCMs typically have a horizontal resolution of 100–600 km. This resolution is quite coarse relative to the scale of exposure in most of the impact assessments (including impact on infrastructures at urban scales). Also, many atmospheric processes (e.g., clouds) and land surface features (e.g., soil and vegetation types) occur at much smaller scales, and hence cannot be properly modeled. Instead, these properties are averaged over the larger scale using the technique of parameterization. This is one of the prime sources of uncertainty in the outputs of GCMs. Moreover, its many mechanisms and processes are not fully understood by the scientific community as whole, and these also induce uncertainty in future projections. However, these are not the two largest sources of uncertainty. In addition to the aforementioned sources of uncertainty, assumptions regarding future emissions of greenhouse gases and aerosols is the largest source of uncertainty. Because it is impossible to quantify this uncertainty mathematically, it is presented as a series of possible emission scenarios or projections. To quantify this uncertainty, a collection or ensemble of climate models is used. Each of these simulations represents an "equally plausible" scenario with the range of future changes, with the ensemble yielding the measure of confidence in any particular change. Hence, different research groups across the globe can make different assumptions, and treat clouds and aerosols different ways. This gives rise to multiple climate models across the globe.

To address this challenge of decision-making under uncertainty, the climate community has standardized a set of climate modeling experiments to compare the different models and improve our understanding of the climate system. This has been termed the Coupled Model Intercomparison Project (CMIP). Climate model results provided the basis for important components of the Intergovernmental Panel on Climate Change (IPCC) assessments, including the understanding of climate change and the projections of future climate change and related impacts. The IPCC's fifth assessment report relied heavily on the output of CMIP5.

According to the IPCC's special report on extremes (SREX)[6]

> It is *likely* that the frequency of heavy precipitation or the proportion of total rainfall from heavy falls will increase in the 21st century over many areas of the globe. It is *virtually certain* that increases in the frequency and magnitude of warm daily temperature extremes and decreases in cold extremes will occur in the 21st century at the global scale. It is *very likely* that the length, frequency, and/or intensity of warm spells or heat waves will increase over most land areas. Average tropical cyclone maximum wind speed is

likely to increase, although increases may not occur in all ocean basins. It is *likely* that the global frequency of tropical cyclones will either decrease or remain essentially unchanged. There is *medium confidence* that droughts will intensify in the 21st century in some seasons and areas, due to reduced precipitation and/or increased evapotranspiration.

Despite the uncertainty that exists in the modeling process, terms such as "likely," "virtually certain," and "very likely" point toward the significant changes in various attributes of weather and climate-related extremes, emphasizing the need for adaptation to reduce the risk because of changes in fundamental attributes of threats.

3.5.2 Changes in Vulnerability and Consequences

IPCC's SREX[6] further highlights that the

changes in extreme events greater impacts on sectors with closer links to climate, such as water, agriculture and food security, forestry, health, and tourism. For example, while it is not currently possible to reliably project specific changes at the catchment scale, there is *high confidence* that changes in climate have the potential to seriously affect water management systems. However, climate change is in many instances only one of the drivers of future changes, and is not necessarily the most important driver at the local scale. Climate-related extremes are also expected to produce large impacts on infrastructure, although detailed analysis of potential and projected damages is limited to a few countries, infrastructure types, and sectors. Increases in exposure will result in higher direct economic losses from tropical cyclones. Losses will also depend on future changes in tropical cyclone frequency and intensity.

3.5.3 Managing Risks of Climate Extremes and Disasters

Adaptation to climate change and disaster risk management provides a range of complementary approaches for managing the risks of climate extremes and disasters. Measures that provide benefits under current climate and a range of future climate change scenarios, called low-regrets measures, are available starting points for addressing projected trends in exposure, vulnerability, and climate extremes. They have the potential to offer benefits now and lay the foundation for addressing projected changes. Potential low-regrets measures include early warning systems, risk communication between decision makers and local citizens, sustainable land management including land use planning, and ecosystem management and restoration. Other low-regrets measures include improvements to health surveillance, water supply, sanitation, and irrigation and drainage systems; climate-proofing of infrastructure; development and enforcement of building codes; and better education and awareness. Effective risk management generally involves a portfolio of actions to reduce and transfer risk and to respond to events and disasters, as opposed to a singular focus on any one action or type of action. Such integrated approaches are more effective when they are informed by and customized to specific local circumstances. Successful strategies include a combination of hard infrastructure-based responses and soft solutions, such as individual and institutional capacity building and ecosystem-based responses.

Let us consider the example we already discussed in section 3.3 but with the due consideration to potential changes in attributes of hazards. We have discussed previously why such change may occur. Let us discuss how we may begin to understand, characterize, and hopefully deal with such change.

Incidentally, there were reports (e.g., in the *Washington Post*) that Harvey was the third 500-year flood that Houston experienced in three years. Some immediate questions for scientists and engineers are the following: (a) What is the chance of three 500-year (0.2%) events occurring in three successive years? (b) When do the probabilities (e.g., in question (a)) get so low that we begin to re-evaluate whether an event of that magnitude can indeed be thought of as a 500-year event anymore (or, whether that event has now grown more frequent, say, a 100-year event)? (c) How can we attribute the change, if any, suggested from question (b) to causal drivers such as urbanization or climate change? (d) What are the implications to risk computations and expected loss? (e) What potentially actionable information, if any, can be fed back to engineers, policymakers, and stakeholders, whether at local, regional, national, or global scales? Interestingly enough, a couple of years before Harvey, scientists reporting their findings in a paper called "Grey Swan Tropical Cyclones" mentioned: "We define 'grey swan' tropical cyclones as high-impact storms that would not be predicted based on history but may be foreseeable using physical knowledge together with historical data."[7] They showed that tropical cyclones may indeed cause unprecedented damage. Indeed, their work showed that

> Grey swan tropical cyclones striking Tampa, Cairns and Dubai can generate storm surges of about 6 m, 5.7 m and 4 m, respectively, with estimated annual exceedance probabilities of about 1/10,000. With climate change, these probabilities can increase significantly over the twenty-first century (to 1/3,100–1/1,100 in the middle and 1/2,500–1/700 towards the end of the century for Tampa). Worse grey swan tropical cyclones, inducing surges exceeding 11 m in Tampa and 7 m in Dubai, are also revealed with non-negligible probabilities, especially towards the end of the century.[7]

Let us consider how to address the questions posed here and the observations in the *Nature Climate Change* paper.

Question 1: What is the chance of three 500-year (0.2%) events occurring in three successive years?

Here, the probability of occurrence of a 500-year event in any given year is 1/500 or 0.002. Hence, the probability of occurrence of three 500-year events in three consecutive years is $(1/500)^3 = 0.0000008\%$.

Question 2: When do the probabilities (e.g., in question (a)) get so low that we begin to re-evaluate whether an event of that magnitude can indeed be thought of as a 500-year event anymore (or, whether that event has now grown more frequent, say, a 100-year event)?

The answer to this question will typically require a statistical test of significance and, where possible, connecting to the underlying physics and/or causal drivers. As the probabilities get lower, we get more and more confident that some fundamental change may have happened or is happening over time. The confidence may be further supplanted if the physics of the system leads us to belief that such change is indeed happening or is very likely to happen. In this specific case, we may consider that a probability of 0.0000008%, as computed in Question 1, is beyond the realm of what may occur owing to natural variability alone. The possibility that the fundamental change may have occurred in the basic attribute of flood extremes in this case is supplanted by our knowledge of urbanization (because increasing urbanization results in more of the rainfall getting converted to floods) and climate change (because a warmer atmosphere and a warmer ocean are more likely to intensify rainfall extremes). Whether the 500-year event has now turned into (say) a 100-year event could potentially be answered by processing observed and numerically model-simulated data through sophisticated methods such as those motivated from extreme value theory.

Question 3: How to attribute the change, if any, suggested from question (b) to causal drivers such as urbanization or climate change?

To answer this question, we will typically require the information about changes in threats, vulnerability, and exposure in a given region. Changes in the attributes of extremes can be evaluated using probabilistic methods such as trend analysis and non-stationary extreme value theory, which use changes in the statistical attributes of observations or climate model outputs (such as general circulation models). Attribution to urbanization requires understanding the changes in land use pattern in the given area. Let us understand this with help of a simple example. As mentioned before, flooding and extreme precipitation events are strongly correlated in the sense that keeping land use and demographics constant, a 100-year flood precipitation will result in 100-year flood levels given that no other trigger of flooding event is present (e.g., tide surge). However, if there are changes in the land use pattern (e.g., change in impervious area over a region), then the exact relationship between flood precipitation may not hold anymore. For example, if there is a net increase in built surface, then the rate and volume of runoff (water that is not absorbed by the soil) will increase. The volume of rainfall that cannot be catered by the drainage system ultimately gives rise to flooding. Using the spatial analysis tools such as geographical information systems in combination with hydrological models (which are used to model the discharge [rate of flow of water] in streams or at given location) and hydraulic models (used to model the depth of floods given discharge), one can predict the expected discharges as a consequence of change in topography and use and compare it to existing flood return levels.

Question 4: What potentially actionable information, if any, can be fed back to engineers, policymakers, and stakeholders whether at local, regional, national, or global scales?

Recall our discussions on fragility, risk, and reliability. Infrastructures and hydraulic infrastructures are often designed to withstand extreme events of certain magnitude. However, if exposed to intense extreme events beyond design tolerance, these systems either fail or lose their intended functionality. Hence, if a structure such as a dam is designed to cater to 200-year flooding event (200-year Return Level denoted by RL200) is exposed to a 500-year event flooding (RL500), the dam is likely to fail if the magnitude associated with RL500 >> RL200. This ratio of return levels RL_T to RL_t is termed extreme volatility index (EVI) and can help in quantifying and visualizing the anticipated surprise caused by intense extreme events.[8] The EVI can take values greater or equal to one. The intuition behind EVI is that it is a design RL for t year's corresponding to which infrastructure system has been designed. If EVI is approximately equal to unity, this implies that a more extreme return level is equal to the design return level, and hence there is less probability of more intense extremes. On the other hand, when this ratio deviates from unity, it implies that when rare extremes occur, they occur with high intensity. Hence, information thus obtained from metrics like these can help to plan for recovery and rescue operations ahead of disaster strikes.

3.6   Risk Management in Non-Stationary Setting

Traditional approaches to risk management in a non-stationary world begin with the null hypothesis that "no trend" is present, with little or no attention to the possibility that we might ignore a trend if it really exists. Concluding a trend exists when it does not, or rejecting a trend when it actually exists, has its implication for decision-making. Rosner et al.[9] provided a rational decision approach in the non-stationary world, where the decision to adapt or not to adapt to changes in extremes is made on the basis of expected regret calculation. Let us understand this approach with the help of an example. To mitigate the risk of flooding in a coastal city X due to anticipated intensification of extremes, the city's mayor is considering the design of an advanced drainage system. The cost of design of such a system will result in a cost of $19 million. The data analytics team working for the city provided the actionable inputs. Now, there are two possibilities:

- Possibility I: At a 95% significance level, data analysts rejected the null hypothesis that the time series of extremes is stationary. The current drainage system will be rendered highly inefficient within the next decade and could result in $25 million in losses as a consequence of intensified flooding scenarios. However, if the drainage system is upgraded, the expected loss can be reduced to $4.4 million. However, if no trend is actually present but statistical experiments report the trends (Type I error: there is 5% of this possibility), an upgraded system will still help in reduction of the losses to $3.6 million.

- Possibility II: Also, there is a 50% chance that if the trend is actually present, but due to poor/limited samples on extreme flooding events or other factors the data team cannot falsify the hypothesis that the trend is not present (Type II error). The expected loss without any adaptation measure in place and without accounting for the upward trend in flooding is expected to be $20.6 million.

All this information is combined to determine the potential damages avoided by adaptation whether or not we experience the trends (or non-stationary world). The damages avoided may not exceed the cost of adaptation for the trend that never materialized. Similarly, we may incur the costs that could have been prevented by implementing an adaptation strategy if a trend that we were not expecting actually materializes. Each of these avoidable costs is termed as a regret and forms the basis of an economic analysis. The resulting decision is thus based on the two measures of expected targets: the expected cost of avoidable damage if we underprepare and the expected cost of unneeded infrastructure if we overprepare. Expected regret of over-preparation is then weighted against the expected regret of underpreparation. Generally, one would recommend investing in adaptation when the expected regret of underpreparation is greater than the regret of overpreparation, and not to adapt otherwise. This information can be presented in the form of a decision tree (Figure 3.4).

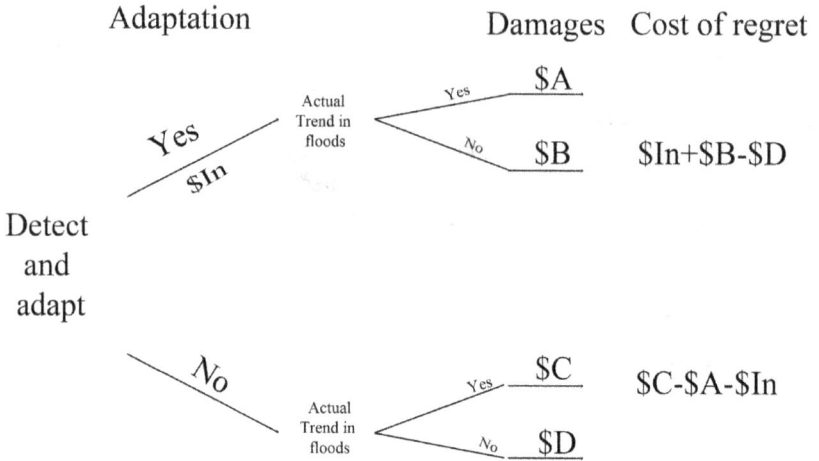

Figure 3.4. Decision tree for regret-cost calculations in a non-stationary world.

In the scenario of overinvestment, regret will only occur if investment is made on the basis of statistical result but no trends are actually present (Type I error, represented by α). Hence, the expected regret of overinvesting is equal to the sum of total investment made and loss that still happens after adaptation. Similarly, in the scenario of overinvestment, regret will only occur if we discarded the trend but it is actually present (Type II error, represented by β). Hence, the expected loss of underinvestment is equal to the total loss incurred due to intensified flood minus losses that would have happened despite adaptation measures in place minus the savings on investment.

Mathematically, the cost of regret for overinvestment is given by $(In + B - A)$, the cost of regret for underinvestment is $(C - A - In)$, and the expected regret for the two scenarios is $(In + B - A) \times \alpha$, and $(C - A - In) \times \beta$, respectively.

3.7   Exercise

Exercise 3.2: Consider the following information that we used for discussion in section 3.5.

The cost of adaptation measures for a positive trend in flooding events will result in a cost of $19 million. The data analytics team working for the city has been assigned the responsibility to provide inputs to aid in decision-making. The result of the data analysis has two outcomes:

- **Possibility I**: At the 95% significance level, data analysts rejected the null hypothesis that the time series of extremes is stationary. The current drainage system will be rendered highly inefficient within the next decade and could result in $25 million in losses as a consequence of intensified flooding scenarios. However, if the drainage system is upgraded, the expected loss can be reduced to $4.4 million. However, if no trend is actually present but statistical experiments report the trends (Type I error: there is 5% of this possibility), the upgraded system will still help to reduce the losses to $3.6 million.

- **Possibility II**: Also, there is a 50% chance that if the trend is actually present, but due to poor/limited samples on extreme flooding events or other factors the data team cannot falsify the hypothesis that the trend is not present (Type II error). The expected loss without any adaptation measure in place and without accounting for the upward trend in flooding is expected to be $20.6 million.

Using the decision tree diagram shown in Figure 3.4, compute the expected regret costs associated with overpreparation and underpreparation. Based on these results, discuss whether investment in adaptation is economically viable or not.

3.8   Conclusions

Conventional risk management frameworks rely on characterization and reliable quantification of hazards. In this chapter, we introduced the concept of hazard classification and hazard identification. Once hazards are identified, the next step that is relevant to inform the risk framework is modeling of a hazard to quantify its intensity and frequency of occurrence. Then, we learned how these models are used for quantification of risk to infrastructure components using convolution equations. The risk models that we have discussed so far are based on the implicit assumption that attributes of hazards, vulnerability, and exposure are stationary and historical observations can serve as a guiding light for the future. However, there has been enough evidence from the last century that hazard, vulnerability, and exposure are no longer stationary and positive trends, and these attributes are likely to persist in the twenty-first century as a result of human-induced climate change and socioeconomic changes. Finally, we outlined how adaptation to climate change and disaster risk management provide a range of complementary approaches for managing the risks of climate extremes and disasters. Now that we are familiar with the advantages and limitations of concept of risk, it is time to tackle the beast! In the next chapter, we will introduce the concept of modeling of infrastructure systems with a special focus on networked infrastructure. We will briefly discuss the limitations of present risk and a reliability-based framework for a complex system, and gradually dive into hazard curve–agnostic ways to quantify resilience.

References

[1] Blaikie, P., Cannon, T., Davis, I., Wisner, B. *At Risk: Natural Hazards, People's Vulnerability and Disasters.* Abingdon, UK: Routledge; 2014.

[2] Rausand, M. *Risk Assessment: Theory, Methods, and Applications.* Hoboken, NJ: J. Wiley & Sons; 2011.

[3] Flood Hazards, Prediction, & Mitigation; n.d. www.tulane.edu/~sanelson/Natural_Disasters/floodhaz.htm (accessed August 31, 2017).

[4] *Science Magazine*, 28 August 2015, p. 9. http://www.sciencemagazinedigital.org/sciencemagazine/28_august_2015?pg=9&lm=1510581487000 (accessed December 5, 2017).

[5] http://www.nytimes.com/1999/09/23/business/business-digest-628689.html.

[6] IPCC. Summary for policymakers. In: Field, C. B., Barros, V. R., Dokken, D. J., Mach, K. J., Mastrandrea, M. D., Bilir, T. E., et al., editors. *Climate Change 2014 Impacts Adaptation, and Vulnerability Part A: Global and Sectoral Aspects. Contribution of Working Group II the Fifth Assessment Report of the Intergovernmental Panel on Climate Change.* Cambridge, UK, and New York: Cambridge University Press; 2014, pp. 1–32.

[7] Lin, N., Emanuel, K. Grey swan tropical cyclones. *Nature Climate Change* 2015; advance online publication. https://doi.org/10.1038/nclimate2777.

[8] Khan, S., Kuhn, G., Ganguly, A. R., Erickson, D. J., Ostrouchov, G. Spatio-temporal variability of daily and weekly precipitation extremes in South America. *Water Resources Research* 2007;43:W11424. https://doi.org/10.1029/2006WR005384.

[9] Rosner, A., Vogel, R. M., Kirshen, P. H. A risk-based approach to flood management decisions in a nonstationary world. *Water Resources Research* 2014;50:1928–42. https://doi.org/10.1002/2013WR014561.

4 Modeling Infrastructure Systems and Quantifying Resilience

4.1 Introduction

The economy of a nation and well-being of its citizens depend on the continuous and reliable functioning of infrastructure systems. The U.S. President's Commission on Critical Infrastructure defines an infrastructure system as "a network of independent, mostly privately-owned, man-made systems and processes that function collaboratively and synergistically to produce and distribute continuous follow of essential goods and services."[1] Further, critical infrastructure systems are defined as those systems whose incapacity or destruction would have a debilitating impact on defense and economic security. Different nations have slightly different lists of critical infrastructure systems, but most include communications, transportation, water supply, government services, and emergency services.

Critical infrastructure systems are not isolated but highly interconnected and mutually interdependent. For example, water and telecommunication systems need a steady supply of electric energy to maintain their normal operations, while electric power systems require the provision of water and various telecommunication services for power generation and delivery.[2] While interdependencies can improve the infrastructure operational efficiency, recent events such as the 2003 North American blackout, 2004 Indian Ocean tsunami, and 2014 South Asian floods have shown that interdependencies can enhance system vulnerability. The damage in one critical infrastructure system can produce cascading failures, sending ripple effects throughout regional or national scales.

On July 30–31, 2012, two severe blackouts hit northern and eastern India, which left around 600 million people without power. Given the size of the population affected, this has been recorded as the world's largest power outage in history. In the summer of 2012, an extreme heat wave and increased demand for water and electricity by the agricultural sector resulted in record power consumption in many parts of the nation. The situation was further exacerbated by delayed monsoons, which resulted in drawing increased power from the grid for running water pumps to irrigate paddy fields throughout the rice-growing belt of North India. On July 30, circuit breakers on the 400kV line between the cities of Bina and Gwalior tripped. As this line fed into another transmission section between the cities of Agra and Bareilly, circuit breakers on this section also tripped. This caused cascading failure throughout the power distribution system, leaving more than half the nation's states without power. The failure also cascaded through other infrastructure systems and severely affected performance of other lifelines and critical infrastructure systems including transportation, water distribution, and wastewater treatment units. More than 300 trains were stalled, leaving passengers stranded. This is one of the classic examples of the "curve of interdependencies," which is a prime feature of infrastructure systems, and how man-made (or technological) events interact with natural events (such as delayed monsoons and heat waves) to give rise to cascading failures across the system.[3,4]

Current risk analysis methods identify the vulnerabilities of specific system components to an expected adverse event and quantify the loss in functionality of the system as a consequence of the event occurring. Application of such frameworks to infrastructure systems and constituting facilities entail comprehensive understanding of intensity, duration, and frequency of hazards, and all possible failure modes through which structure can fail when exposed to threat or hazard. In Chapter 2, we demonstrated an application of Probabilistic Risk Assessment to a simplified problem on failure of structure due to flooding. Application of risk management has focused on hardening of specific components to withstand the identified threats to an acceptable level and to prevent overall system failure. However, with increasing interconnectivity across social, technical, and economic networks, systems are getting increasingly complex, hence making risk analysis of individual components cost-prohibitive.[5] Also, the uncertainties associated with the vulnerabilities of these systems, combined with the unpredictability of climatic extremes, challenges our ability to understand and manage them. To address these challenges, risk analysis should be used where possible to help prepare for and prevent consequences of foreseeable events, but resilience must be built into systems to help them quickly recover and adapt when adverse events do occur. A roadmap for enabling the development of such capability requires (1) methods to define and measure resilience, (2) new modeling and simulation techniques for highly complex systems, (3) development of resilience engineering, and (4) approaches for communication with stakeholders. It should be noted that resilience is not a substitute for risk management or principled design that we discussed in Chapter 2. In fact, resilience is a complementary attribute of adaptation and mitigation that can aid the traditional risk framework. Risk management helps the system prepare and plan for adverse events, whereas resilience management goes further by integrating the capacity of a system to absorb and recover from adverse events and then adapt. This chapter covers the various aspects of infrastructure modeling and resilience quantification, including techniques to model complex infrastructure networks exemplified through regional and local infrastructure systems, using infrastructure models to understand cascading interdependencies across infrastructure systems, and finally methods to quantify resilience.

In the first section, the modeling techniques for critical infrastructure networks (both isolated and interdependent) are covered, with detailed discussions and examples on network science methods. In the second section, we will discuss cascades of failure in interdependent system. Finally, in the third section, we will go through a few case studies to understand how critical infrastructure networks have been impacted globally by natural and man-made perils, and how enabling resilience in the conventional risk framework has the potential to minimize the damage and expedite recovery after disasters.

4.2 Modeling Critical Infrastructure Systems

Modeling and simulation of complex, interconnected socio-technical systems allow system managers to identify weak spots, plan countermeasures in advance, and prepare in advance for diverse and heterogeneous threats and vulnerabilities. Growing complexity and the emergence of unprecedented and unpredictable threats demand sound principles, innovative thinking, databases, models, methods, and simulations of socio-economic technical systems, and the application of systems theory and network science in resilience analysis. Once the system is defined and models to support resilience quantification are developed, the next step is to design interdependent infrastructures to be more resilient. Unlike risk-based design, which focuses on one component at a time, resilience engineering identifies critical system functionalities that are valuable to stakeholders and society. It also involves the development of customized socio-technological methods and solutions to ensure these functionalities are sustained under broad categories of threats. Thus, resilience engineering builds resistance, adaptability, and the ability to recover quickly in the face of adverse events.

The existing modeling and simulation approaches that are used to model critical infrastructure facilities are broadly grouped into the following categories: [6]

1. Network-based approaches

2. System dynamics–based approaches

3. Agent-based approaches

4. Empirical approaches.

In this chapter, we will briefly introduce these approaches and will cover network science–based approaches in more detail with application on a simple toy network and real-world infrastructure system (i.e., Indian Railways Network as examples).

1. **Network-based approaches**: Critical infrastructures (CIs) are described by networks, where nodes represent different critical infrastructure system components, and links represent the physical and relational connections

among them. This representation provides intuitive representations along with the detailed descriptions of their topology and flow patterns. Performance response of critical infrastructure to hazards can be analyzed by first modeling the failures from hazards at component levels and then simulating the cascade failures with and across critical infrastructure systems. In the past two decades, network science methods for infrastructure modeling have gained a lot of popularity, as these methods are generalizable for infrastructure systems with varying complexity operating at disparate spatial scales. For example, network science methods have been used to understand the resilience of systems ranging from global air transportation networks to regional power distribution systems to urban scale water distribution systems. Network science methods are broadly grouped into topology-based methods and flow-based methods.

Topology-based methods model the CI systems only based on their topologies, with the discrete state of each component (represented as a node or link) and usually with two states: normal and failed. These components can fail directly from hazards, or indirectly due to isolation from the rest of the network. The performance of networks is measured by many metrics, such as the number of failed or normal components before and after hazards, loss in connectivity, inverse characteristic path length, connectivity loss, and metrics related to the size of the largest connected cluster in the network. Topology methods are further subdivided into analytical methods and simulation-based methods.

In analytical methods, CIS topologies are often modeled without considering the distinction between source, transmission, and sink nodes. Each CIS is characterized by degree distribution and size of the largest connected component. The results of analytical analysis yield the performance response of the network in form of generalizable equations, but these equations are generally applicable to randomly constructed networks of large or infinite size. However, real infrastructure systems operate with spatial constraints and have limited size. Also, in the analytical method, it is often assumed that various components fail with the identical probabilities under random failures or targeted attacks, which is not the case with real-life networks.

In simulation methods, CIS are modeled by their topologies with additional consideration of node heterogeneity. With the availability of more and more data, simulation methods are gaining popularity and often aid in validating the generalizable results obtained from analytical methods. Performance of each network is measured by many metrics, such as the number of normal or failed components, the inverse of path length, the connectivity loss, the redundancy ratio, and the largest component-related metrics. Also, these methods enable incorporation of some functional properties of nodes and edges such as duration of the component unavailability, number of customers served, and system-level performance (such as lost service hours). These metrics facilitate the assessment of mitigation actions, such as hardening the individual component performance and deciding the recovery sequence after perturbation.

Both analytical and simulation-based methods have been applied to both independent and interdependent systems. For example, Gao et al. developed the analytical framework to study the performance response of n interdependent networks under random hazards;[7] Barabási et al. developed a set of analytical equations to assess the robustness and resilience of single networks.[8] Similarly, simulation-based methods have been used to quantify resilience of single networks such as the Indian Railways Network,[9] and the U.S. National Airspace System, as well as interdependent systems such as Boston's power distribution and mass transit system.[10]

Flow-based approaches take account of the services or flows made and delivered by the CIS, in addition to topological information. Nodes and edges constructing the infrastructure topologies have the capacities to produce, load, and deliver the services. For example, in a transportation network, this movement will correspond to flows, and services will correspond to desired level of these flows, and these flows take place along the edges connecting various nodes. Any perturbation in the form of random failure, a targeted attack, or a natural hazard results in a change in flow through nodes or edges, and thus a change in network performance can be measured as a function of time. We cover network science–based methods in more detail in the next section with examples using Gephi.

2. **System dynamics–based approaches**: System dynamics–based approaches use a top-down method to manage and analyze complex adaptive systems involving single and interdependent systems. Feedback, flow, and stock are the basic concepts in these types of approaches. Feedback approaches indicate the connection and direction of effects between CIS components. Stock represents quantities or state of the system, the levels of which are controlled over time by flow rates between stocks. System dynamics approaches model the infrastructure systems using two diagrams: a causal-loop diagram capturing causal influence among different variables, and a stock-and-flow diagram describing the flow of information and products through the system. The critical infrastructure protection/decision support system (CIP/DSS) tool is one such example of a system dynamics approach for infrastructure modeling. It uses about 5,000 variables to model all infrastructure systems as defined by presidential directive (see Chapter 1) and their interdependence at aggregate level. It enabled decision makers to determine what consequences might be expected from disruptions to infrastructure, explore mechanisms behind the consequences, and evaluate mitigation to particular risk. CIP/DSS has been used to study a variety of scenarios, such as

analyzing the cascading effect of a power system disruption on the tele-communications systems, and predicting the impact of displacement of people due to natural catastrophes. System dynamics approaches capture important causes and effects under a disruptive scenario, capture the effects of policy and technique factors to reflect the system evolution in the long term and provide investment recommendation, and help build consensus on the investment priorities among stakeholders.

The limitations of such approaches include the following: (1) as the causal-loop diagram is established based on the knowledge of a subject-matter expert, it is also semi-quantitative and depends upon the knowledge of that subject-matter expert; and (2) many system dynamics approaches use differential equations to describe the system level behavior, so cali-brating the associated parameters and determining these equations in the first place is a non-trivial task.

3.   **Agent-based models**

Agent-based models have been used to model infrastructures and their interdependency. Agent-based approaches adopt the bottom-up method and assume the complex behavior emerges from many individual and relatively simple interactions of autonomous agents. Each agent interacts with the other and its environments using a set of rules, which mimics the way a real counterpart of the same type would react. For example, the Critical Infrastructure Modeling System (CIMS) tool developed by the Idaho National Lab has been used to analyze the cascading effects and conse-quences associated with critical infrastructure interdependencies through a 3D graphical representation. CIMS models the Critical Infrastructures System (CIS) topology in detail and provides decision makers the ability to visualize interdependencies and damage effects of events. However, when the CIS sizes and complexity increase, the visual analysis methods may not suffice.

Agent-based approaches model the behaviors of decision makers and the main system participants in the critical infrastructures, and enable the capture of all types of interdependencies among the systems. However, this type of method has some weaknesses: (1) the quality of simulations is highly dependent on the assumptions made by the modeler regarding agent behaviors, and these assumptions may be difficult to justify statisti-cally or experimentally; (2) calibrating the simulation parameters is a challenge; and (3) gathering the validation data for various scenarios is a non-trivial task, as most of the agencies keep this information classified or confidential.

4.   **Empirical risk methods**

Empirical risk methods rely on historical failure data and expert experi-ences. These methods are used to identify the vulnerability of critical infrastructures and minimize their risk to non-functionality or reduced functionality during hazards. Using the information from the previous occurrences of hazards and disasters, a cascade diagram is plotted to describe the cascading failures process across critical infrastructures under a specific initiating event. The frequency of an initiating event, the probabilities of all involved events, the number of people being affected, and the duration of each subsequent event are determined based on historical data and expert judgement. The result of such an exercise is a time-dependent cascading failure tree showing each failure event and its impact on infrastructure expressed in terms of qualitative measures such as null, low, medium, or high.

The empirically based risk analysis largely depends on the empirical data and expert judgements. A small sample size can result in erroneous and misleading insights.

4.3   Hands-On: Network Science–Based Methods

In this section, we will learn about network science methods to model critical infrastructure systems in more detail using the Indian Railways Network (IRN) (Figure 4.1) and a toy network (Figure 4.2) to illustrate various concepts.

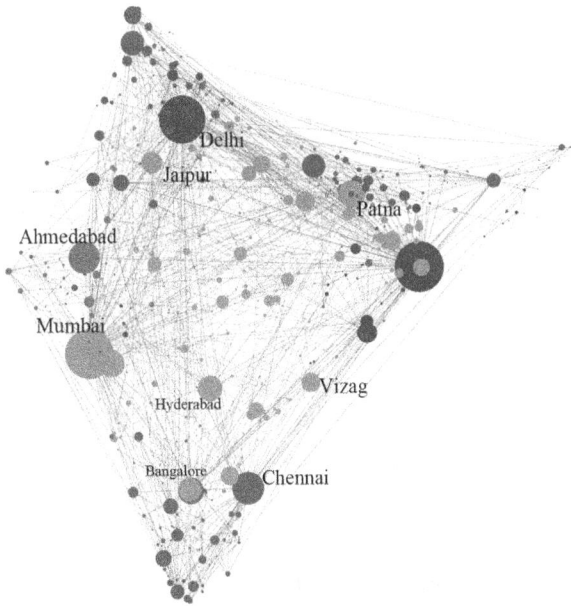

Figure 4.1. Network representation of the Indian Railways Network. The origin destination of IRN comprises 809 nodes and 2,422 links. The size of the node is representative of the traffic the given node is handling.

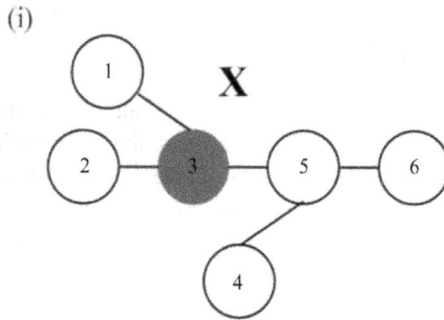

Figure 4.2. Toy network with 6 nodes and 5 links.

4.3.1 Background

Indian Railways Network (IRN) is the world's largest network in terms of passenger kilometers per year (passenger kilometer/year is the product of passenger per year times length of railroad in kilometers). The IRN is among the most important lifelines in India. It transports more than 8.4 billion passengers annually and has played an important role in the nation's economy as well as in relief and rescue operations after both man-made and natural hazards. For example, after 2013's Cyclone Phailin, the IRN played an important role across the eastern coast of the nation. Given the economic and societal importance of this network, it is indeed the lifeline of the world's second largest nation by population, and hence we will use the data from IRN to learn network modeling.

4.3.2 Definitions and Terminology

Before we dive into the method and system details, let us get familiar with a few concepts/terms that we have used so far in discussions. We will use IRN data to understand various terminologies and concepts.

The first step in network modeling is to identify the system or network itself. A network is defined as a collection of a system's components, called vertices or nodes, and the direct interactions between them, termed as links or edges. In IRN, nodes represent the railway stations, and two nodes are considered to be connected if there is at least one direct train running between the two stations.

> **The number of nodes**, N, represents the number of components in the system. In IRN, there are 809 stations with at least one originating or terminating train. Thus, $N = 809$.
> **Number of links**, L, represents the total number of interactions between the nodes. For IRN, $L = 2{,}422$.
> **Directed versus undirected**: A network is said to be directed if there are links associated with direction. It is called undirected if links are not associated with a particular direction. For IRN, because we are

modeling network as an origin-destination network, links are not associated with any direction, and hence it is modeled as undirected.

Degree and average degree: Degree, denoted with k_i, represents the
number of links it has to other nodes. For example, node X of the network shown in Figure 4.2 has a degree of 3. The average degree
represents the average of the degree of all nodes in the network.

Question 1: What is the average degree of the network shown in
Figure 4.2?

Degree Distribution: Degree distribution provides the probability that a
randomly selected node in the network has degree k. For a network
with N nodes, the degree distribution is given by:

$$p_k = \frac{N_k}{N} \tag{4.1}$$

Degree distribution is central in network science methods in network characterization and robustness studies. Cumulative degree distribution gives the
probability that a node has more than K connections to other nodes and is
given by:

$$P(k > K) = 1 - \sum_{k\_min}^{K} p(k) \tag{4.2}$$

The cumulative degree distribution of IRN is shown in Figure 4.3.

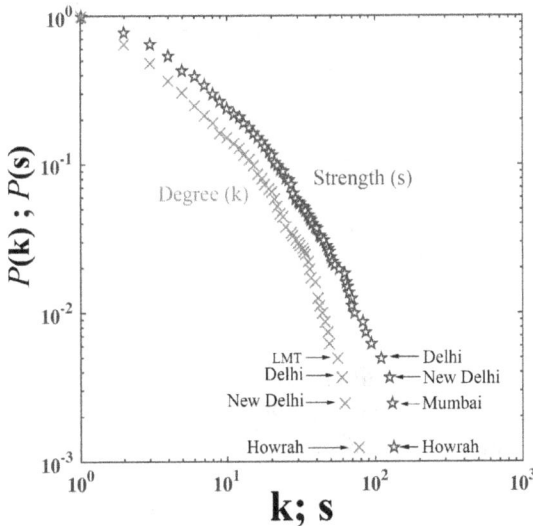

Figure 4.3. A cumulative probability distribution of node degree and strength
(weighted degree) on log-log scale. Distribution follows the truncated power
law, where most stations have a small number of connections, with the excep-
tion of a few hubs.

Source: [9]

Adjacency matrix: As a result of perturbation, nodes or edges of the network are likely to be affected. To keep track of such changes, a complete list of interactions within the network is generated. For mathematical purposes, this information is often presented in the form of an adjacency matrix. The adjacency matrix of a directed network of N nodes has N rows and N columns, and its elements being:

A_{ij} = 1 if there is a link pointing from node j to node j, and zero otherwise

The degree of the node i can be obtained directly from the elements of the adjacency matrix. For an undirected network, a node's degree is a sum over either the rows or the columns of the matrix.

For the network shown in Figure 4.2, the adjacency matrix will have a size of 6 × 6:

$$A_{ij} = \begin{bmatrix} 0 & 0 & 1 & 0 & 0 & 0 \\ 0 & 0 & 1 & 0 & 0 & 0 \\ 1 & 1 & 0 & 0 & 1 & 0 \\ 0 & 0 & 0 & 0 & 1 & 0 \\ 0 & 0 & 1 & 1 & 0 & 1 \\ 0 & 0 & 0 & 0 & 1 & 0 \end{bmatrix}$$

Using the adjacency matrix, one can determine the degree of individual nodes, average degree, number of links, number of nodes, and size and number of connected components of the network. These metrics are important as these help in determining resilience and recovery characteristic of the network.

Example 4.1

For the network shown in Figure 4.2, determine the degree of individual nodes, average degree, and number of links using the adjacency matrix.

Solution

a.   **The degree of individual nodes** is the sum of all the elements along rows or columns. For example, for node 1, degree = 1; for node 3, degree = 3; and so on.

b.   **Number of links**: The total of all elements of A_{ij} divided by 2. Division by 2 is done to correct for double counting, as the link between nodes i and j is the same as the link between nodes j to i in an undirected network. Thus L = 10/2 = 5.

c. **Average Degree**: The sum of the degree of all nodes/number of nodes = $(1 + 1 + 3 + 1 + 3 + 1)/5 = 2$

Weighted network: So far, we have just described the network links in binary terms. However, in real-world networks, flow through nodes and links is also important as it is used as a proxy of services flowing in the network. For example, in IRN, this flow is measured in terms of number of trains; for the global air transportation system, weights are measured in terms of number of passengers; in the water distribution system, it is the rate of water supplied to households and industries and so on.

For weighted networks, the elements of adjacency matrix carry the weight of the link as:

$$A_{ij} = w_{ij} \tag{4.3}$$

Shortest path: The shortest path between two nodes is the path with the fewest number of links. The shortest path is often called the distance between nodes i and j, and is denoted by d_{ij}. If a node gets detached from the network, then the shortest distance between the node any other node of the connected node is infinity.

Network diameter: It is the largest distance recorded between any pair of nodes. For smaller networks as shown in Figure 4.5, the network diameter can be calculated by visual inspection. However, for networks with large number of nodes, algorithms such as breadth first search is generally used.

Connectedness: An infrastructure network (or any other lifeline) is of limited use if it cannot deliver supply and services from one point to another. For example, in IRN, if stations exist in isolation, it would be impossible for trains to deliver goods and services and transport people from one city to another. Hence, the key utility of most of the infrastructure systems is to ensure connectedness. In an undirected network, two nodes i and j are connected if there is a direct path between them. A network is connected if all pairs of nodes in the network are connected. That is, in a connected network, we can reach any other node starting from a given node. Thus, the connected component of a network is a subnetwork in which any two nodes are connected to each other by paths, and the component with the largest number of nodes is termed as the largest connected component. A fully connected network will have the size of the largest connected component equal to the number of nodes itself. Once nodes or edges are removed from the network, isolated nodes or isolated clusters of nodes begin emerging in the network, and hence the size of the largest connected component keeps reducing. After removal of a certain fraction of nodes f, the size of the largest connected cluster approaches zero, and that is when the largest component vanishes and many isolated clusters emerge in the network.

State of network functionality: To quantify network performance, we need to define some measures of functionality that account for connectivity or service flow in the network. In this example, we use the size of the largest connected cluster to measure the functionality of the network. Total functionality (TF) is the network number of nodes in the largest component when network is fully functional. In this case, the number of nodes in such a cluster is 752, hence TF = 752. When one or more stations are incapacitated by disruption, the size of the largest connected cluster reduces and networks begin to fragment. The number of stations in the largest cluster is termed as Fragmented Functionality (FF). The state of network functionality is thus defined as the measure of fractional functionality to total functionality (FF/TF). This state of critical functionality (SCF) is always between (both inclusive) zero and 1.

Centrality measures: Centrality identifies the most important nodes in the network. Centrality indices are answers to the question, "what characterized an important vertex?" Because word importance has a wide number of meanings, there are as many definitions of centrality. A few examples of such measures include degree centrality, closeness centrality, betweenness centrality, and eigenvector centrality.

Degree centrality (or importance by number of connections) is the number of links incident upon an edge.

Closeness centrality is the average length of the shortest path between the node and all other nodes in the graph. The more central a node is, the closer it is to all other nodes.

Mathematically,

$$C(x) = \frac{1}{\sum d(i,j)} \tag{4.4}$$

Where $d(i, j)$ is the shortest path between nodes i and j.

Betweenness centrality is a centrality measure that quantifies the number of time a node acts as a bridge along the shortest path between two other nodes. The betweenness of a node is computed in the following way:

- For each pair of nodes (i, j), compute the shortest paths between them.
- For each pair of nodes, determine the fraction of shortest paths that pass through a node under consideration. Let us say B.
- Sum this fraction all over pair of nodes.

Mathematically,

$$C_{b(B)} = \sigma_{ij}(B)/\sigma_{ij} \tag{4.5}$$

Where σ_{ij} is the number of shortest paths from node i to node j.

Eigenvector centrality assigns the measure of the influence of a node in a network. It assigns relative scores to all nodes in the network based on the concept that connections to high-degree nodes receive higher rank.

4.3.3   Network Visualization

Once we have defined the network, the next step is visualizing the network. Here, we will use the network visualization tool, Gephi (https://gephi.org/) to visualize the Indian Railways Network and measure various characteristics associated with the network. The two files used in this tutorial are uploaded in the repository.[11] The file *datawithlatlong.csv* contains the names of the stations and their latitudes and longitudes. An index column is used to make the csv file compatible for reading in the software. The file *Edgesweighted.csv* stores the information about edges. Source is the origin of the edge, and Target indicates the termination of an edge. Weight indicates the number of trains/day running on an edge.

- Once Gephi is installed on your machine, you can import the network data from the .csv file. Before we do that, it is recommended to install the various plugins (especially GeoLayout) to visualize the spatial networks (Tools > Plugins).

- Once plugins are installed, select File>New Project.

- The next step is to import the data. Select Data Laboratory>Import Spreadsheet and select the node file. From the drop-down menu, change the "As Table" option to Nodes table. Click Next.

- In the next window, change LAT and LON to double (specifies datatype as decimals), and Index to integers.

- To import edges, select Data Laboratory>Import Spreadsheet and select the edge file. From the drop-down menu, change the "As Table" option to Edges table. Click Next. Make sure that Weight is specified as Double or Integers. Click Finish.

- Now, we have imported the data. The next step is network visualization. Click on Overview and you should be able to see an entangled web of nodes and edges. For meaningful visualizations, we will use GeoLayout. In the Layout dialogue, select GeoLayout from the drop-down menu and change the scale to 9,000. Scale controls how the nodes are separated from each other, and one can experiment with various attributes of GeoLayout.

- Next, we will compute the various network attributes (Average Degree, Average Weighed Degree, Connected Components, Network Diameter, etc.) using the Statistics window.

- Once the attributes are computed, we can use these for network visualization. Under Appearance, select the node size using the Size icon (Figure 4.4). Select Ranking> Degree and Apply. You should see a few large nodes on the network. These are the nodes with large degrees and are

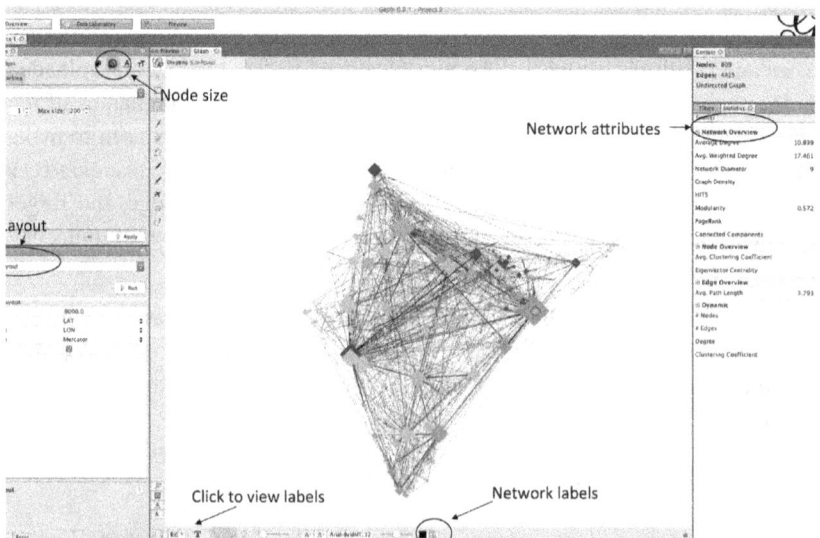

Figure 4.4. Network analysis and visualization in Gephi.

called hubs. You can play with other appearance options (such as color of nodes, size of nodes, color of text) in the same window.

- To enable labels on the figure, you can select the various labeling options from the Attributes icon. Once required attributes are selected, click on Show Node Labels and you should be able to see the selected attributes on the map.

- To simulate the effects of perturbation on the network, you can delete the nodes either by deleting the nodes from Data Laboratory or using the node Editor. After deleting a fraction of nodes, network attributes are computed again and the impact of various hazards on the network can be quantified. These simulations are discussed next.

- You can inspect the results of analysis under Data Laboratory once network attributes are computed.

4.3.4 Simulating Hazards

Network visualization is the first step in in network-based methods to model infrastructure. The intact network gives us various measures which can then be used as benchmarks to quantify the impact of various events on the infrastructure systems. Because the probabilities of failure of various nodes were not known, we assumed that if a particular node falls in the impacted area it is in a failed state, and it is working otherwise if it is connected to any other node in the network. For example, we simulated the impacts of three hazards on IRN: the 2004 Indian Ocean tsunami, the 2012 power blackout, and simulated cyber physical attacks (Figure 4.5). In the simulation inspired by the tsunami, 9% of the stations were removed along the eastern coast. Similarly, we simulate a scenario based on a cascade from power grid, similar to fallout from the 2012 blackout during which at least half the Indian states lost power, and it percolated to the IRN resulting in halting of trains. Finally, a hypothetical cyber or cyber physical attack is simulated which impacted the top 3% of stations in decreasing order of degree. A list of the stations removed during these three events appears in Table 4.1.

After removing the stations, we recomputed the network performance indicators, and we measured the size of the largest connected cluster after the three hazards, which are 679, 641, and 669. Given that there were 752 nodes in the largest connected cluster, the SCF after each event can be computed as 679/752 (0.90), 641/752 (0.85), and 669/752 (0.89) for tsunami, blackout, and cyber physical attack, respectively.

This is one example of a performance indicator. Recall the various performance metrics introduced in Chapter 2. There is no consensus on the choice of which performance indicator should be chosen for particular infrastructure systems, but it is context dependent and depends upon what questions we are seeking to answer.

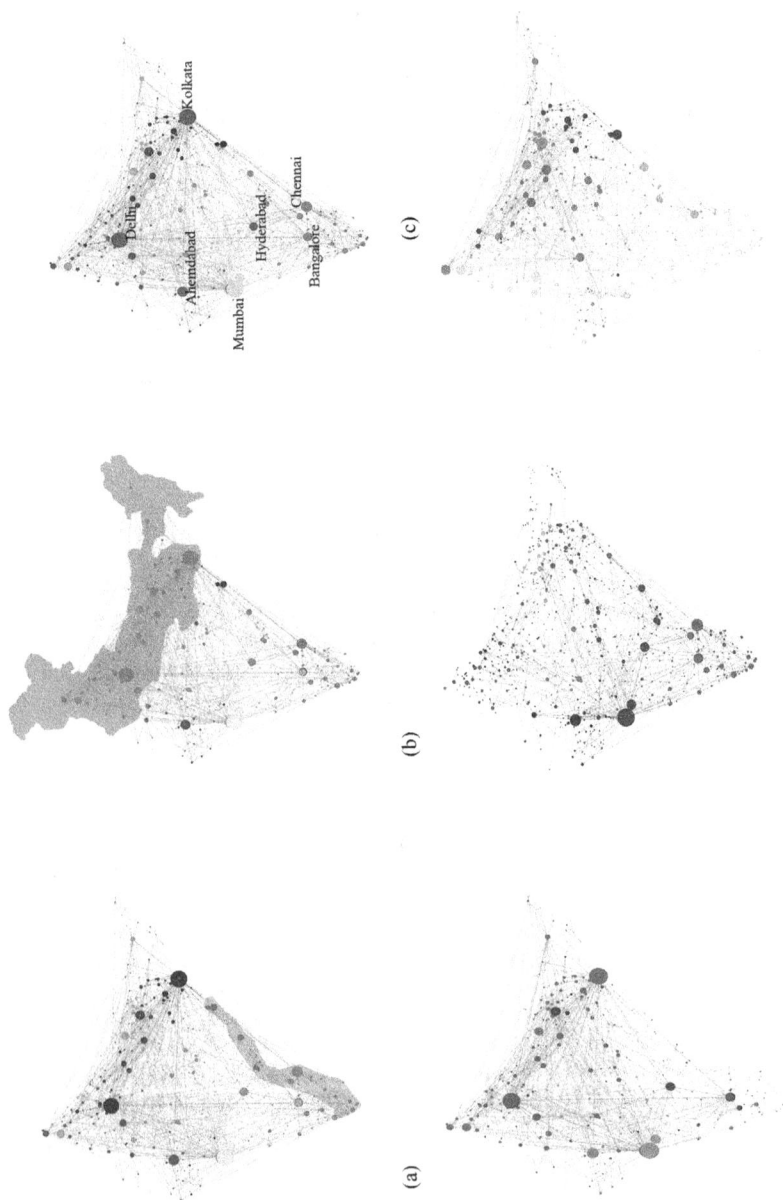

Figure 4.5. Simulating the impact of realistic natural and man-made hazards on IRN: (a) 2014 tsunami; (b) 2012 power blackout; (c) simulated cyber-physical attacks.

Source: [9]

Tsunami	Power Failure	Cyber Physical
Bhubaneswar	Ajmer	Ahmedabad
Chennai Central	Ambala Cant	Bangalore City
Chennai Egmore	Amritsar	Chennai Central
Cuttack	Anand Vihar	Chennai Egmore
Ernakulam	Asansol	Delhi
Gudivada	Bareilly	H Nizamuddin
Guntur	Bareilly City	Howrah Jn
Kanyakumari	Bikaner	Hyderabad Decan
Kochuveli	Danapur	Jaipur
Kollam Jn	Darbhanga	Kacheguda
Machilipatnam	Delhi	Kolkata
Madurai	Delhi S Rohilla	Lokmanyatilak
Mayiladuthurai	Dibrugarh	Mumbai
Nagercoil	Dibrugarh Town	New Delhi
Narasapur	Firozpur Cant	Pune
Puducherry	Ghaziabad	Sealdah
Puri	Gorakhpur	Secunderabad
Rameswaram	Guwahati	Shalimar
Sengottai	H Nizamuddin	Yesvantpur
Tiruchendur	Howrah	
Tiruchirapalli	Jaipur	
Tirunelveli	Jammu Tawi	
Tirupati	Kamakhya	
Trivandrum	Kanpur Anwrganj	
Tuticorin	Kanpur Central	
Vijayawada	Kolkata	
Villupuram	Lal Kuan	
Visakhapatnam	Lucknow	
	Muzaffarpur	
	New Delhi	
	New Tinsukia	

Tsunami	Power Failure	Cyber Physical
	Palwal	
	Patna	
	Pratapnagar	
	Puri	
	Sealdah	
	Tinsukia	
	Varanasi	

Table 4.1. List of the stations removed for each of the three hazards.
Source: [9]

4.3.5   Quantifying Resilience

Going by NIAC's definition of resilience that we introduced in Chapter 1, the performance response of an infrastructure system can be divided into three stages. The first stage is the disaster prevention stage from normal operation to the onset of failure in the system. In the case of the IRN and tsunami example, this phase represents the normal operations of IRN before the tsunami hit the eastern coast. The first stage represents the resistance capacity of the system and its ability to absorb risk. The second stage is the damage propagation stage after initial failure. This is often termed as the rate of loss of functionality. The second stage is the damage propagation process after initial failure. It reflects the absorptive capacity of the system as the degree to which it absorbs the impact of initial damage and minimizes the consequences, such as cascading failure. The third stage is the recovery process, during which system damage information is collected for damage assessment, and resources are allocated for repair or repair sequences are determined for faster and efficient restoration.

The three stages together constitute a typical infrastructure response to disruptions. The first stage mainly focuses on the local level impacts, translating hazards into component-level failures. The second stage emphasizes system-level effects, translating initial component-level failure to system-level failures. The third stage characterizes the restoration response, translating external efforts into system repercussions.

Hazard-Centric Resilience Quantification

In such frameworks, a hazard is treated as one of the central components of the framework, and system performance is expressed as a function of hazard intensities. Expected annual resilience of the system (AR) in such frameworks is defined as the mean ratio of the area between the real performance curve and the time axis, the area between the target/ideal performance curve (without perturbations) and time axis [12]. Mathematically,

$$AR = E\left[\frac{\int_{o}^{T} P(t)dt}{\int_{o}^{T} P_{o}(t)dt}\right] \tag{4.7}$$

where $P(t)$ is the actual performance curve; $TP(t)$ is the target performance curve, which can be constant line or a stochastic process; and T is the time duration (generally, 1 year or 365 days). If N events are occurring in a given year, the equation can be elaborated as:

$$AR = E\left[\frac{\int_{o}^{T} P(t)dt - \sum_{n=1}^{N(T)} AIA_{n}(t_{n})}{\int_{o}^{T} P_{o}(t)dt}\right] \tag{4.8}$$

where n is the event occurrence number; t_{n} is the occurrence time of the nth event, and $AIA_{n}(t_{n})$ is the area between the real performance curve and the targeted performance curve, termed the impact area. For practical applications, target performance is generally a constant line. Hence, $\int_{o}^{T} P_{o}(t)dt$ represents a rectangle with area of $TP \times T$, where TP is targeted performance. Note that this performance can be measured using performance metrics of relevance (see Chapter 2). Hence, AR can be expressed as:

$$AR = E\left[\frac{T \times TP - \sum_{n=1}^{N(T)} AIA_{n}(t_{n})}{T \times TP}\right] = \frac{TP - E(\frac{1}{T}\sum_{n=1}^{N(T)} AIA_{n}(t_{n}))}{TP} \tag{4.9}$$

Impact area is a random variable that is highly uncertain and is a function of hazard type, initial damage level from hazard, the maximum impact level from hazard, the restoration time, and the restoration cost. It is non-trivial and sometimes improbable to determine the exact form of $AIA_{n}(t_{n})$ before the occurrence of the hazard, and hence statistical assumptions are made regarding the analytical form of the same. One of the most common assumptions is to model the hazard occurrence as a Poisson process, with rate of occurrence (parameter of distribution) v^{h}, where h represents the hazard type. Under this assumption, $E\left(\frac{1}{T}\sum_{n=1}^{N(T)} AIA_{n}(t_{n})\right)$ for a single hazard can be approximated as $v^{h}E[AIA^{h}]$, where $E[AIA^{h}]$ is the expected impact area under hazard type h accounting for all possible hazards. When generalized for all possible hazards, $E[AIA^h]$ takes the following complex form:

$$E\left[AIA^h\right] = \sum_{q^h} E\left(AIA^h\left(q^h\right)\right)\phi^h(q^h) \qquad (4.10)$$

where $E(AIA^h(q^h))$ is the expected impact area under a given hazard intensity q^h, and $\phi^h(q^h)$ is the probability of occurrence of hazard intensity q^h.

While frameworks like these put the entire resilience framework into quantitative perspective, this advantage comes at a cost. Estimating and validating the form of probability distribution of hazard intensity takes us back to the hazard curve estimation that we discussed in the last chapter. Even if the functional form probability density or mass function that the probability of occurrence of hazard will assume, determination of parameters associated with hazards is challenging for complex systems. Moreover, determining $AIA^h(q^h)$ and $\phi^h(q^h)$ for unforeseen and non-stationarity events is improbable, and stationary assumptions often yield misleading insights.

The promising way to overcome this problem is to focus on the system instead of speculating on possible threat probabilities, and direct attention to all possible failure modes, and use the worst possible scenario to decide the most efficient recovery. One example of such approach is discussed next.

Network-Based Approaches to Quantify Robustness and Recovery

To quantify the resilience of Indian Railways, in addition to the three scenarios mentioned above, we consider another scenario where a network loses its entire functionality to identify the network's response to targeted attacks and random failures (often termed as robustness) and identify the most important nodes throughout the network to expedite the recovery. We measure the change in SCF as stations are removed in (a) decreasing order of degree, (b) decreasing order of node traffic volume, and (c) random order. Given the predominant hubs in the network as we identified in Figures 4.2 and 4.3, the network loses its critical functionality steadily as soon as these hubs are removed. In fact, removal of only 20% nodes in decreasing order of degree will result in cessation of the existence of a giant cluster. On the other hand, IRN is relatively robust to random failures, and the giant cluster will cease to exist after removal of 80% nodes.

Once a network loses its functionality, the next step is to restore the essential functionality in the most efficient way. To decide the restoration sequence, one of the intuitive ways is to identify the importance in using network centrality measures that we defined earlier. Degree centrality and weighted degree centrality are direct measures of station connectivity and traffic volume, respectively. On the other hand, betweenness centrality is the measure of the average number of times any passenger traveling between origin-destination station pairs needs to go through the station under consideration; closeness centrality measures the station's proximity, while eigenvector centrality is a proxy of importance of stations because of its connections. For performance comparison of various restoration strategies, the rate of strategic restoration is compared with random restoration (an average of 1,000 random recovery sequences).

In this case, IRN recovery is most efficient at most stages of partial or full recovery when betweenness centrality is chosen as for generating a recovery sequence. The efficiency of each recovery sequence is measured by computing its corresponding Impact Area (IA), which is defined as the area between the recovery curve and the y-axis representing SCF. Hence, a smaller IA signals a more efficient recovery strategy. On average, random recovery sequences have an IA (averaged over $N = 1,000$ random sequences) that is at least 250% larger than the betweenness centrality–based sequence. The betweenness centrality–based sequence also has a 67% smaller IA than the sequence based on connectivity (degree) (Figure 4.6).

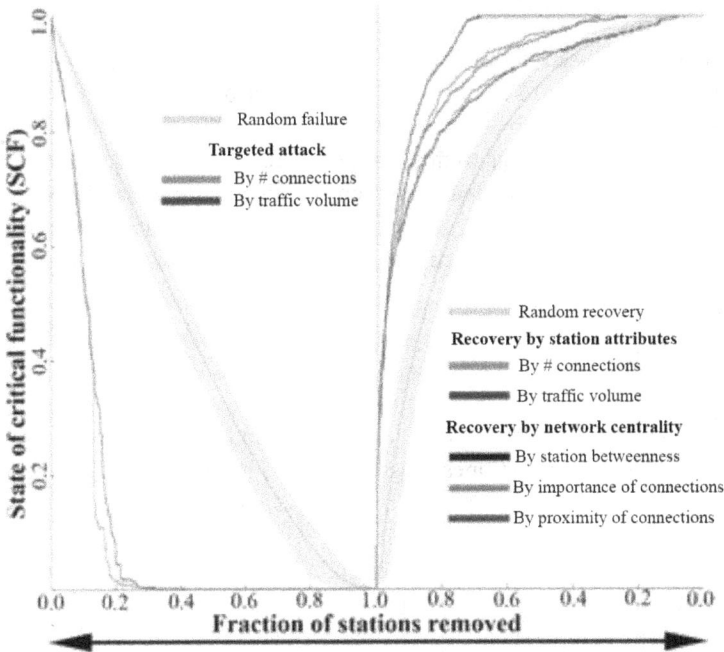

Figure 4.6. Robustness and recovery of the Indian Railways Network.
Source: [9]

4.4   Network-Performance Assessment

In the last section, we studied one example of the use of network science for quantification of resilience. Given the popularity that these network science methods have gained, researchers have used network-performance indicators that consider either the topology or functionality of networks while keeping them tractable for practical applications. Topology relates to how the arrangement of components, such as electrical substations in power grids or bridges in road networks, affects network performance. Although topology-based measures provide useful information, they are not sufficient for practical applications alone. In practice, desirable performance measures should also quantify the changes in network functionality during normal operation and contingencies. Metrics discussed in this section have been adapted from the work of Ghosn et al.[13]

4.4.1   Topology-Based Performance Metrics

In topology-based methods, lifeline networks are represented as an abstract network with a set of N nodes and a set of K edges. The connections between each pair of nodes are represented by an $N \times N$ adjacency matrix A, whose element is equal to 1 if there is connection between node i and node j, and zero otherwise. Once this network structure is imposed, network measures of connectivity and efficiency can be used to assess the performance of infrastructure system. The ability of a network to keep its connectivity after being subjected to hazard events is often assessed by the connectivity loss (C_L) metric. Denote N_G as the number of connecting paths from every generation or supply node of a lifeline system to any of its N_D distribution or consumption nodes. Also, denote N_i^g as the number of generation units able to supply flow to distribution node i after a disruption. Then, C_L can be calculated as:

$$C_L = 1 - 1/N_D \sum_{i=1}^{N} \frac{N_i^g}{N_g} \tag{4.11}$$

where the averaging is done over all distribution nodes of the network, and the flow through transmission lines is assumed to be bidirectional. This metric is useful for most lifeline systems with clearly established source and demand nodes or regions. However, when dealing with other more distributed layouts, such as transportation or telecommunication systems, most nodes act as both travel sources and destinations, so adaptations are required. Another important metric to evaluate network-performance topologically is network efficiency (E).

$$E = \frac{1}{N(N-1)} \sum_{i \neq j} 1/d_{ij} \tag{4.12}$$

where d_{ij} is the shortest path between nodes i and j. E measures how efficient the communication between different nodes in the network is on average.

4.4.2   Flow-Based Functional Performance Metrics

In addition to topology, infrastructure systems such as water distribution, transportation, and electricity play an important role in the transmission of water, traffic, and energy, respectively. Thus, it is important to establish performance metrics that combine network topology with flow patterns. Service flow reduction (S_{FR}) and related metrics consider flow capacity after a disruptive event, as well as supply/demand constraints in an optimization framework. The S_{FR} metric determines the amount of flow that a damaged network can provide compared to what it provided before damage.

$$S_{FR} = 1/N \sum_{i=1}^{N} D_i / A_i \qquad (4.13)$$

where D_i denotes the actual amount of flow through node i after disruption, A_i represents the flow through the node before disruption, and N is the total number of nodes in the network.

Although the principles behind topological and flow-based performance metrics apply to different types of networks, differences in the timescales and operational requirements necessitate specialized adjustments to make such metrics implementable in specific industries. Hence, examples of metrics used in the performance evaluation of power, water, and transportation networks today are presented next.

4.4.3   Metrics for Power Distribution Networks

Power distribution networks are becoming critical portions of lifeline systems because their performance influences other infrastructure networks, and their study is less advanced than that of power transmission systems. For example, the extended loss of electric power at the distribution level— where transmission-level systems are often energized more expeditiously than distribution systems—could affect water distribution systems, telecommunication systems, and traffic systems, in addition to the functionality of essential facilities. Hence, power network performance can be evaluated using a number of criteria related to topology and flow, and measured at various hierarchical levels. Examples of performance measures at the bulk level include the difference between power supply after a hazard and that under normal operational conditions (i.e., residual power supply), or the time required to restore high-voltage networks (i.e., time to restoration). In addition, there are some customer-based measures that integrate technical and socioeconomic dimensions, such as the percentage of households without power after hazard and the reduction of regional gross product (RGP). In relation to customers, the Institute of Electric and Electronic Engineers established several service reliability metrics related to the number of customers affected by outages registered at the power distribution system level, but whose root cause can be anywhere in the system. These include the system average interruption duration index (SAIDI), system average interruption frequency index (SAIFI), and customer average interruption duration index (CAIDI), among others. These metrics are widely used by utility operators and can be defined as

$$SAIDI = \frac{\sum \text{customer hours off for each operation}}{\text{total number of customers served}}$$

$$SAIFI = \frac{\sum \text{customer hours off for each operation}}{\text{total number of customers served}}$$

$$CAIDI = \frac{SAIDI}{SAIFI} \tag{4.14}$$

Utilities use these metrics to establish annual operational reliability targets, and are starting to use probabilistic methods to determine which events constitute outliers from normal operation. These outliers, or major event days (MED), are important to separate normal operation from extreme event operation and address reliability at two operational regimens. However, a link between target performance reliability at the customer level and structural performance at the facility or equipment level still needs to be established, as well as links between distribution-level customer metrics and transmission-level performance metrics, including loss of load probability (LOLP) or energy not supplied (ENS).

4.4.4   Water Distribution Networks

Performance of water distribution networks (WDNs) can be defined in terms of the probability that the system is operational (reliability); the percentage of time that the system is operational (availability); or in terms of surrogate measures that reflect the operational requirements of the system (serviceability). "Reachability" in WDNs is often a performance index, which indicates the probability that a certain amount of water flow would reach key locations (nodes). As in power networks, researchers have also proposed customer-based (and flow-based) metrics for water networks. These include the volume of unserved demand, the number of days of water outage, the number of customers interrupted, and the ratio of the served demand to the total demand. Other measures focus on the damage of components in the system.

Metrics for Transportation Networks

As with most lifeline systems, early research on transportation networks assessed the performance of individual components such as a road segment, a bridge, or a tunnel independently. In one of the earliest studies, topology-based measures to evaluate the seismic performance of entire highway networks have been used, with the total number of highway sections open, total length of highway open, and total weighted "connected" length of highway open to account for the inherent uncertainties in evaluating network performance, the concept of probabilistic fully connected ratio (FCR), which is defined as the ratio of the number of samples where all nodes are reachable to the total number of samples. Among simple flow-based performance indicators that can be used in a deterministic or probabilistic fashion, travel time is defined as the time spent to reach a destination by all the users that depart within a fixed time window.

4.5 Interdependent Infrastructure Systems: Case Study

Infrastructure systems such as power distribution, communications, transportation networks, and water distribution networks are highly coupled and intertwined, and operate as system of systems. While this independency aids in swift and efficient operations across the systems (imagine the functioning of communication systems without electricity!), this independency comes at the cost of fragility.[2,4,7] Let us understand this fragility with the help of an example of power distribution system and power supply in the Greater Boston area. In a power distribution network, substations (usually represented as nodes in the network) are sensitive to overload, and if removed, it results in the redistribution of loads over the remaining network. This load distribution can trigger overloading events across the network, leading to cascading failures (similar to the sequence of events during the 2012 India power blackout). The effect is further amplified when interdependent networks are removed from the network, leading to a new redistribution of the loads and ultimately to cascading failures. When a node in one network depends in a node in the other network, the failure of the latter can induce failure in the former (Figure 4.7).

In the present case, the transportation system depends on a power distribution system for running trains and maintaining other functionalities within stations. Hence, a failure in power distribution results in cascades of failures in Boston's mass transit system (MBTA). Boston's subway operates on four

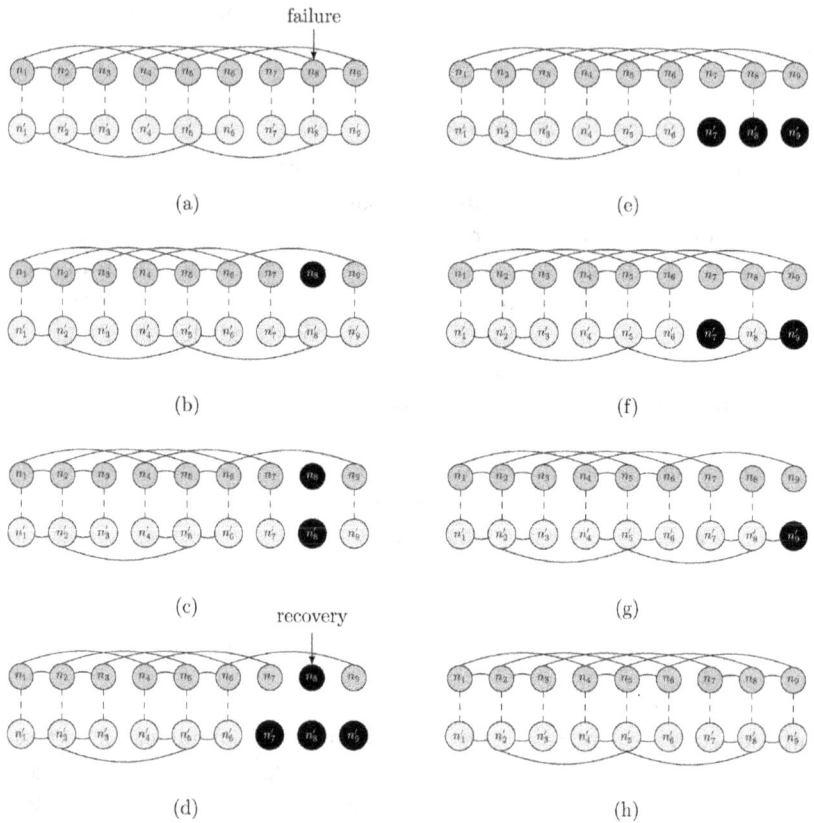

Figure 4.7. Network response model. The functioning nodes are represented in lighter shades in the two networks; malfunctioning nodes are represented by black; (a–d) show component cascading failure starting at node ns; (e–h) show component stepwise recovery starting at node n_8.

Source: [10]

lines—red, green, blue and orange—running radially between Boston and its environs. As both power distribution and transportation can be represented as networks, we used a topology-based network method to model both infrastructure systems. For MBTA, a pair of stations is considered to be connected if there a direct train between the pair. In a power distribution system, two substations are connected if there is a direct physical connection between them. While data about MBTA is publicly available through maps, data about power distribution systems is often kept secured. Hence, we simulated the network using statistical attributes of the U.S. power grid (Figure 4.8).

Also, one-to-one dependency is considered between transportation and power distribution system, which means that each transportation node has its

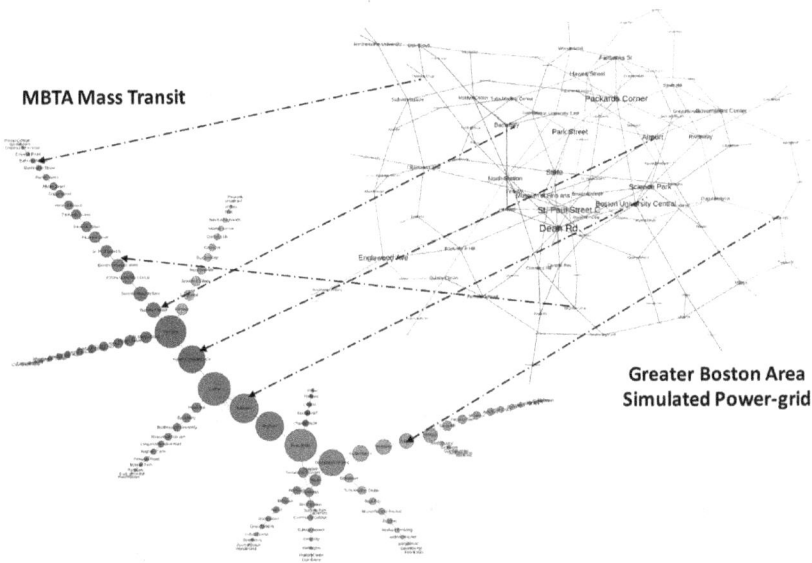

MBTA Mass Transit

**Greater Boston Area
Simulated Power-grid**

Figure 4.8. Complex network representation of (left) Boston's subway system with 121 nodes and 124 links and (right) power distribution network with 121 nodes and 184 links. Unidirectional arrows connecting the two systems are an illustrative representation of the dependence of the transportation system on the power distribution system.

Source: [10]

own power supply. To understand the network response, we considered two scenarios: the January 2015 snowstorms and hypothetical system-wide outages. The performance of the entire system can be measured using single multiple metrics as discussed in previous section. However, in the absence of data about the number of consumers affected, network topology–based measures are a reasonable choice.

For 100% functionality loss, the hypothetical scenarios are considered: (1) random failure in MBTA, (2) targeted failure in MBTA in decreasing order of traffic volume through the station, and (3) random failure in the power grid. Results suggest that the random failure in the dominant network (power grid) proves as debilitating as a targeted attack on the dependent network (transportation network) (Figure 4.9), highlighting the curse of interdependency.

During the 2015 snowstorms, approximately 23% of MBTA stations were severely impacted, but it resulted in the loss of around 80% functionality across the system. Once disrupted, network recovery rates based on centrality-based metrics are measured, and it is observed that recovery by a station's location in the network would result in a better recovery response.

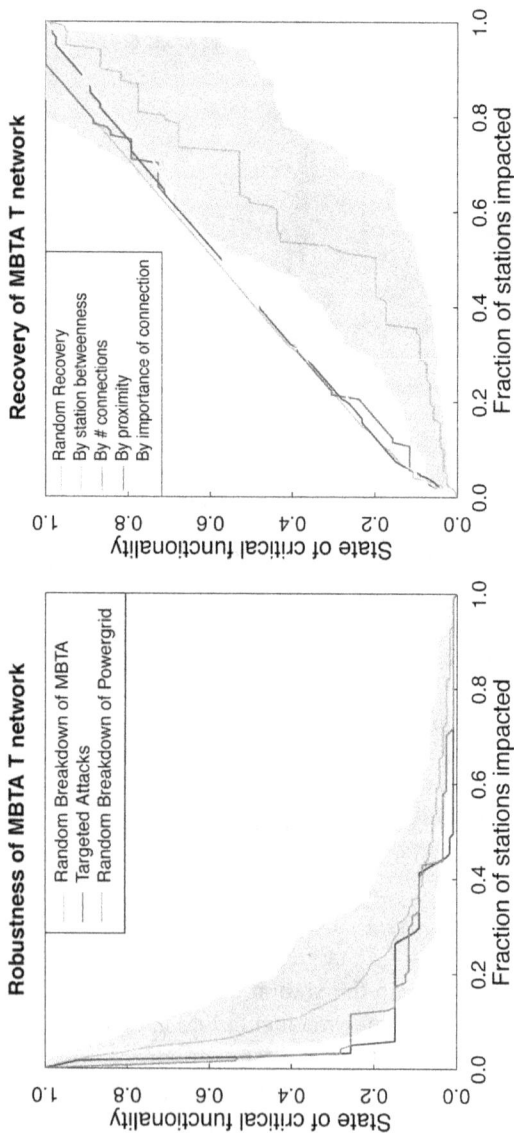

Figure 4.9. Robustness (left) and recovery (right) characteristics of MBTA subway network for random and targeted failures of the subway system and random failures in the power grid. Once 100% MBTA stations are perturbed, recovery is done using various network centrality measures, with random recovery as a benchmark for the performance comparison of strategic restoration.

Source: [10]

4.6   Resilience Principles

Most of the approaches to quantify system performance that we have discussed so far are reactive in the sense that these measures quantify the changes in system after perturbation. However, the emerging paradigm of resilience emphasizes the proactive perspective, that is, considering events prior to encounter with the threat.

If a current system is not resilient, there are features that need to be added to the system to make it resilient. The principles to build resilience within the systems are broadly categorized as physical and process–based principles.

- *Absorption*: The capability of the system to withstand design-level disruption.
  - Hardening: The system should be resistant to deformation.
  - Margin: Increasing the design level (such as by use of factors of safety) to allow for a cushion.
  - Context spanning: The system should adhere to the principle of risk-based design that accounts for various performance levels.
  - Limited degradation: The absorption capacity should not be allowed to degrade due to aging or poor maintenance.

- *Graceful degradation*: If exposed to rare events with high magnitudes, the system should be able to maintain limited functionality even if the system has been destroyed or rendered inoperative, and lose its functionality in such a way that once the event is over, the system can be restored in minimal time with minimum resources.

- *Restructuring*: The system should be able to restructure after encounter with a threat.

- *Reparability*: The capability of a system to repair itself.

- *Functional redundancy*: Two or more independent and functionally different ways to perform a critical task.

- *Physical redundancy*: Two or more independent and physically different ways to perform a critical task.

- *Loose coupling*: The system should have the capability of limiting cascading failures by intentional delays.

- *Reduce hidden interactions*: Potential harmful interactions within and across the systems should be reduced.

Most of these principles are abstract concepts, meaning that their practical adaption goes beyond the traditional prowess of traditional engineering fields and involves changes in policy, governance, incentive structures, and decision-making. These enabling frameworks are discussed in more detail in the next section.

4.7   Exercises

Exercise 4.1: For the toy network shown in Figure 4.2, compute the network efficiency using Equation 4.12 in (a) the normal state and (b) after removing node number 3.

[**Hint**: Here, $n = 6$; the distance between nodes 1 and 3 = 2; the distance between nodes 1 and 2 = 1; the distance between an isolated node and any other node in the connected network is infinity].

Exercise 4.2: For the toy network shown in Figure 4.2, consider the following flow information between the nodes. Nodes 1 and 3: 3 units; nodes 2 and 3: 2 units; nodes 3 and 5: 6 units; nodes 5 and 6: 2 units. As a consequence of disruption, there is 50% reduction in flow on each edge. Assuming the links are bidirectional, compute the change in performance of network using Equation 4.3.

4.8   Conclusion

Natural, engineered, and social systems are growing ever more complex and interconnected. Rapid and often seemingly erratic change, including that caused by humans, is becoming the new normal. A 2009 National Academies Press report observes that continued use of the same decision-making processes, construction methods, and operational practices "as those used in the 20th century will likely yield the same results: increasing instances of service disruptions, higher operating and repair costs, and the possibility of catastrophic, cascading failures."[14] Conventional risk analysis methods, such as Probabilistic Risk Assessment (PRA), focus on the identification of the vulnerabilities of specific components to an expected adverse event and quantify the loss in functionality of the system because of these events. However, strong coupling that exists between social, technical, and economic systems makes this form of protection unrealistic and cost-prohibitive. Because interconnectedness is ubiquitous to these systems, a new paradigm of resilience enabled by network science has been proposed. In addition to acting as connective tissues across built, natural, and social systems, network science tools provide us a way to understand robustness and recovery of these systems in a hazard-agnostic way. However, translating this paradigm to address real-world problems is still a momentous challenge for decision makers, engineers, and social scientists. This new paradigm of resilience can both encapsulate and offer benefits from applications of traditional PRA frameworks. The new insights obtained from real-world applications of resilience frameworks can inform the existing gaps to be bridged to enable integration of resilience in system design and regulatory structures.

References

[1] https://fas.org/sgp/library/pccip.pdf.

[2] Buldyrev, S. V., Parshani, R., Paul, G., Stanley, H. E., Havlin, S. Catastrophic cascade of failures in interdependent networks. *Nature* 2010;464:1025–8. https://doi.org/10.1038/nature08932.

[3] Bhatia, U., Traylor, A., Moskos, C., Blumenfeld, L., Bressler, L., Hall, T., et al. Climate hazards and critical infrastructures resilience. *Encyclopedia of GIS*. Berlin, Heidelberg: Springer; 2015.

[4] Vespignani, A. Complex networks: The fragility of interdependency. *Nature* 2010;464:984–5. https://doi.org/10.1038/464984a.

[5] Linkov, I., Bridges, T., Creutzig, F., Decker, J., Fox-Lent, C., Kröger, W., et al. Changing the resilience paradigm. *Nature Climate Change* 2014;4:407–9. https://doi.org/10.1038/nclimate2227.

[6] Ouyang, M. Review on modeling and simulation of interdependent critical infrastructure systems. *Reliability Engineering & System Safety* 2014;121:43–60. https://doi.org/10.1016/j.ress.2013.06.040.

[7] Gao, J., Buldyrev, S. V., Havlin, S., Stanley, H. E. Robustness of a network of networks. *Physical Review Letters* 2011;107:195701. https://doi.org/10.1103/PhysRevLett.107.195701.

[8] Albert, R., Jeong, H., Barabási, A.-L. The Internet's Achilles' heel: Error and attack tolerance of complex networks. *Nature* 2000;406:200.

[9] Bhatia, U., Kumar, D., Kodra, E., Ganguly, A. R. Network science based quantification of resilience demonstrated on the Indian Railways Network. *PLOS ONE* 2015;10:e0141890. https://doi.org/10.1371/journal.pone.0141890.

[10] Sela, L., Bhatia, U., Zhuang, J., Ganguly, A. Resilience strategies for interdependent multiscale lifeline infrastructure networks. *American Society of Civil Engineers* 2017:265–72. https://doi.org/10.1061/9780784480847.033.

[11] https://github.com/udit1408/Recovery_algorithm.

[12] Ouyang, M., Dueñas-Osorio, L., Min, X. A three-stage resilience analysis framework for urban infrastructure systems. *Structural Safety* 2012;36–37:23–31. https://doi.org/10.1016/j.strusafe.2011.12.004.

[13] Ghosn, M., Dueñas-Osorio, L., Frangopol, D.M., McAllister, T.P., Bocchini, P., Manuel, L., et al. Performance indicators for structural systems and infrastructure networks. *Journal of Structural Engineering* 2016;142:F4016003. https://doi.org/10.1061/(ASCE)ST.1943-541X.0001542.

[14] Council NR. Science and Decisions: Advancing Risk Assessment. 2008. https://www.nap.edu/catalog/12209/science-and-decisions-advancing-risk-assessment. https://doi.org/10.17226/12209.

5 The Future of Critical Infrastructure Resilience

Policy Aspects

5.1   Introduction

The United States entered the twenty-first century with a vast inventory of critical infrastructure, including:

> 55,000 community drinking water systems; 30,000 wastewater treatment and collection facilities; 4 million miles of roads; 117,000 miles of rail; 11,000 miles of transit lines; 600,000 bridges; 26,000 miles of commercially navigable waterways; 500 train stations; 300 ports; and 19,000 airports.[1]

Much of that infrastructure is aged, oversubscribed, and in many cases, further strained by inadequate funding for service life maintenance and upgrades. In addition, age and cost have also hindered investments that might make the systems more resistant to twenty-first-century threats and vulnerabilities. The 2013 National Infrastructure Advisory Council (NIAC) report states that "resilience is especially important in the lifeline sectors—energy, communication, water, and transportation—because they underpin the most essential functions of business, government, and communities."[2]

   In Chapters 1 through 3, we learned that infrastructure systems are spread across various geographical scales. Single hospital buildings, urban transit systems, interstate road networks, the electrical grid, and the global airport network are examples of infrastructure systems operating at disparate scales. Because critical infrastructure systems each operate within varying political jurisdictions, advancing measures that make infrastructures more resilient involves much more than engineering and technical solutions. Infrastructure systems each involve unique sets of public and private stakeholders, owners, and operators. Stakeholders in these infrastructure systems are both internal and external. For example, consider an example of a power distribution system for an urban region. Internal stakeholders are those with an employment, ownership, and investment interest in the system's operations. These entities include power generation and distribution companies, public utility unions, and public and private investors. External stakeholders are those who derive a benefit from the successful functioning of the system. These include customers, creditors, shareholders, and the society. Because internal stakeholders are concerned about various factors such as profitability, business sustainability, and normalcy in day-to-day operations, these factors are the primary drivers for their decision-making. In the absence of a regulatory requirement to do so, internal stakeholders typically will not communicate in advance with external stakeholders to develop joint disaster management protocols. Not surprisingly, this contributes to catastrophic impacts and extends the recovery times for interdependent systems after unforeseen events. During Hurricane Sandy in 2012, the metro New York region experienced this problem. The damage to the port and the subsequent disruption of the maritime transportation system led to a shortage of liquid fuels such as gasoline and diesel to operate emergency vehicles and backup generators. The advancement in understanding resilience from a science and engineering perspective must be complemented by an awareness of the role of public policy in supporting greater coordination and collaboration among infrastructure sectors and across political jurisdictions. In this chapter, we will discuss various impediments that must be overcome to make resilience an operational concept.

5.2   Impediments Affecting Resilient Practices

First, the majority of public and private sector stakeholders do not recognize how unprepared they are to handle foreseeable risks or to respond to uncertainties arising from the complex interdependencies associated with infrastructure systems. Instead, they overestimate their individual capacities to respond to challenges as they arise and have a bias that discounts the risks associated with our aging infrastructure and cyber threats, as well as leading indicators of large-scale disruptive events in our future. A preoccupation with extracting greater efficiencies and reducing costs for legacy and new infrastructure translates into systems that are at a great risk for failing badly during extreme events.

Second, stakeholders lack an integrative approach to advancing resilience across interlocking critical infrastructure systems. In the absence of a widely accepted consensus on what is required to make a system-of-systems resilient, stakeholders rely on approaches derived from localized success stories in disparate domains for discrete hazards. Too often resilience engineering research efforts focus on individual assets. As a result, too little understanding or insight informs the design parameters necessary for system- or network-wide resilience.

Third, stakeholders lack adequate incentives to create resilience. There are few rewards for invested in robustness and redundancies, and in too many cases there are actually penalties. Public and private infrastructure owners have become skilled at transferring risk to someone else and not working collaboratively to take risk on directly. Further, there is a lack of widely accepted measures that demonstrate relevant resilience attributes that markets can reward.

Public and private sector stakeholders lack appropriate frameworks for managing organizational and governance issues on a regional scale. Transport, communications, energy, and water infrastructure systems with increasingly embedded cyber vulnerabilities sprawl across local, state, and national jurisdictions. Ownership and operations are public and private, large and small, and both highly regulated and loosely regulated. This translates into incompatible rules and protocols across the network of organizations and stakeholders, inhibiting local actions.

5.3   Future of Critical Infrastructures Resilience

The future of critical infrastructure resilience will require us to pursue four areas of effort concurrently:

1.   We must bolster expert and public understanding of the resilience imperative and advance resilience by design.

2.   We must devise new measures and rewards that support the appropriate public and private decisions for making sound risk management choices.

3.   We must devise new governance structures if we are to advance critical infrastructure resilience.

4.   We must build resilience skills among professionals who work as a part of national enterprises and agencies.

From a technological perspective, best practices in resilience are likely to be fundamentally different within the next several decades. In the interim, one intriguing possibility is the potential to repurpose existing and emerging capabilities in new ways that enhance hazards resilience. For example, social media made it possible for volunteers to organize their efforts to undertake boat rescues of stranded homeowners in Houston, Texas, after the 2017 flooding associated with Hurricane Harvey. When tasked with identifying novel ways to move essential workers should a hurricane cause widespread damages to the transportation system in the Boston area, a class of graduate students from Northeastern University recommended that the Massachusetts Port Authority consider putting in place contracts with tour operators who use amphibious "Duck Boats." In this way, assets built for tourism could be temporarily repurposed for moving port and airport employees around and across flooded roadways. Evacuation of displaced people during hazards might also benefit by capitalizing on recent developments in the hospitality industry such as Airbnb. When damage from a disaster prevents patients from being transported to hospitals for care, they can be supported by advancements in telemedicine. Furthermore, robotics and drone technologies may also help to rapidly inspect the post-disaster condition of critical infrastructure, mitigating the need to deploy emergency responders to conduct these damage assessments. In all these instances, the potential for new or repurposed technologies to enhance resilience will need to be supplemented with and supported by innovative regulatory principles or structures, financial instruments, and governance or policy mechanisms.

In order to widely deploy new designs of engineered systems, there will have to be incentives in place that encourage the adoption of these designs. These could include market-based drivers such as reduced insurance premiums for infrastructure owners who adopt best practices. Other financial instruments that help drive investments in mitigation measures include catastrophe bonds and resilience bonds. Alternatively, new codes and regulations could be implemented that mandate mitigation measures.

However, current public policies are actually working against the adoption of new resilience measures. Ironically, the reliable provision of public funding for rebuilding in the aftermath of a disaster ends up have the unintended effect of discouraging upfront investments in preparedness. If infrastructure owners know they can count on public assistance when disaster strikes to make them whole, they will be more inclined to live with risk.

An additional disincentive arises from governance structures that are fragmented by jurisdictional, functional, organizational, institutional, and political (local, state, and international) barriers. System-level preparedness, emergency management, and recovery strategies are difficult to devise in such a convoluted policy environment. Stakeholders, end users, or infrastructure facility owners and operators care about their own optimization functions, which may not always align with system-level objectives.

Resilience best practices of the future need to enable the virtuous cycle as depicted in Figure 5.1. A critical momentum is needed to prevent from plunging into a vicious cycle of economic disincentives, policy myopia, and social inertia, resulting in stagnation of engineering and science, to a virtuous cycle of resilient infrastructures, climate preparedness, sustained economic growth, social justice, and greater security.

5.3.1   Bolstering Expert and Public Understanding

The first overarching imperative for advancing critical infrastructure resilience is that we must bolster expert and public understanding of the resilience imperative and advance resilience by design: there is a widespread lack of awareness of the vulnerabilities and consequences of inadequate investments in infrastructure resilience. This situation has resulted, in part, from the twentieth-century orientation toward creating "invisible infrastructure," that is, infrastructure systems that exist in the background so that users only need to be mindful of accessing their benefits. When major disruptions to infrastructures happen, it is essential to have both a rich understanding and deep involvement in response and recovery. As such, establishing greater "infrastructure awareness" among public officials and the general public before disasters strike and systems fail, is an important goal.

Vicious Circle:
Cycle of Under-Preparedness and Disruptions:
Vulnerability to Change Worsened by Uncertainty
Fragility to Disruptions Amplified by Connectivity

Virtuous Circle:
Cycle of Sustained Growth under Adversity:
Action under Uncertainty Aids Adaptation to Change
Managing Interdependence Improves Resilience

Figure 5.1. A vicious cycle of economic disincentives and stagnation in novel engineering or best practices may be caused by a lack of adequate understanding of the interactions among climate stressors, stressed infrastructure systems, and impacted communities and institutions. Societal consensus based on risk and resilient informed decisions and understanding can transform communities and infrastructures to a virtuous cycle of sustained growth.

Advancing infrastructure awareness requires acknowledging three imperatives:

First, decision makers have a hard time assessing resilience if they cannot "see" it. Their decisions before, during, and after disruptive events will therefore benefit from the development of a system-of-systems virtual environment, with state-of-the-art interacting infrastructure network models, that are married with immersive visualization to include:

- **Data** about engineering systems, geospatial features, and user demographics
- **Validated models** of infrastructure operation, user behavior, and the physical environment
  - **Visualization tools** for analysis and planning which support the ability of owners and operators to pose "what-if" questions and see how they will play out.

A second imperative for advancing critical infrastructure resilience awareness is to provide operators with access to data mining and aggregation tools that provide them with data about systems that impact their own operations, so that they can maintain a *margin of maneuver* during event cascades.

A third imperative is to advance awareness at the community level during a stress event by way of crowdsourcing of data about the local conditions and making them available through a mesh network that is grid- and internet-independent, allowing citizens to communicate and empowering them to act as part of a "whole of community" approach.

In short, new modeling and visualization tools are needed to help support both top-down and bottom-up societal efforts to improve resilience. Old and new threats, including those arising from cyber and climate change, can trigger cascading effects that compromise the essential foundations for our society and economy. Decision makers need better tools for anticipating, mitigating, and coping with future disruptive events.

Fortunately, situational awareness, anticipatory information, and practice tools are being transformed by:

- *Computer technologies for games and exercises*: Enabling technologies for war-gaming, tabletop exercises, and what-if simulations, as well as adversarial and game theoretic models.

- *Geographic information sciences and engineering*: The management exploration and analysis of heterogeneous geographic information, multiscale simulations and analysis that are "geography-aware," and incorporation of social media and citizen science along with associated uncertainties.

- *Machine learning and agent-based modeling*: Data-intensive sciences such as knowledge discovery from databases, data mining, information theory, nonlinear dynamics, graphical models, nonlinear physics, signal processing, computational statistics, and econometrics, as well as data-driven simulations such as what-if simulations including agent-based models.

Linking these tools together in innovative ways will enable a greater awareness of risks and how best to manage those risks by allowing researchers, stakeholders, and homeland security enterprise practitioners to better understand the policies, practices, designs, and operations that support and increase resilience.

Social media can be harnessed to cut down on uncertainty following major disruptive events by providing better situational awareness of what is happening in near real time, and support actions by empowered citizens which will significantly alleviate the stress being put on lifeline infrastructures so that it will be easier to speed the recovery of those infrastructures. The potential for crowdsourcing to support and enhance situational awareness during and after a crisis can come from constructing a reliable, decentralized cyber environment in which citizens can continue to communicate and take actions to support one another in ways that relieve stress on broken or disrupted infrastructure.

Along with bolstering understanding among experts and the general public, the future of critical infrastructure resilience will depend on advances in engineering resilience by design. The field of engineering faces a major transformation. In the face of considerable uncertainty, engineers are being called upon to anticipate a variety of major man-made and naturally occurring disruptions as they design infrastructure.

In 2009, the National Research Council (NRC) identified five change drivers that U.S. infrastructure systems must accommodate:

- Economic competitiveness

- Declining U.S. dependence on imported oil

- Global climate change

- Environmental sustainability

- Disaster resilience.

The NRC also highlighted that:

> Although critical infrastructure systems were built as standalone entities for specific purposes, in actuality they are functionally interdependent. For example, power is needed to treat and pump water, water is needed to cool power and telecommunications equipment or to power steam systems, and telecommunications systems provide automated control for transportation, water, wastewater, and power systems.[3]

Because lifeline infrastructures are interdependent, major shocks are likely to result in cascading consequences. But old engineering practices, some embedded in building codes and standards, often fail to acknowledge these interdependencies. They also rarely account for the trade-off issues associated with preparedness in the face of multiple hazards. Looking ahead, future designs for critical infrastructure resilience will need to harvest the insights from a variety of state-of-the-art engineering approaches to include earthquake and hurricane risk mitigation, flood control, climate adaptation, terrorism, and cyber threats.

Testing concepts and innovative design features will require:

1.   Complex network models that provide a unifying framework for natural, engineered, and human systems to describe hazards, model resilience, and enable human-infrastructure interactions.

2.   Simulation models and empirical analysis of network flows with stochastic optimization methods at local and regional scales that characterize network chokepoints and help in disaster preparedness for multiple hazards.

3.   Proactive design of cyber physical lifeline networks for management of cascading interdependent failures that provide new resilient strategies for key infrastructure components and systems, and enable human-cyber-infrastructure interactions.

In conclusion, the creation of critical infrastructure systems that are resilient to multiple hazards will require a systematic exploration of the "design space" that shapes the structure, organization, and function for lifeline infrastructure systems. Of specific interest is embedding concepts from risk-informed performance-based engineering and flexible design to account for uncertainty, surprise, and enhanced adaptation, with the overarching goal of reducing the risk and consequences of cascading failure on interdependent infrastructure sectors.

5.3.2   Rewards and Incentive Measures

A second overarching imperative for advancing critical infrastructure resilience is the need to devise new measures and rewards that support the appropriate public and private decision for making sound risk management choices. Scientists and engineers can develop breakthrough technologies, designs, and applications for bolstering infrastructure resilience, but they are unlikely to be widely adopted in the absence of a business case for doing so. Indeed, many public and private infrastructure owners have become skilled at transferring risks to someone else rather than taking them on directly. They have felt compelled to respond to market drivers that emphasize reducing costs by identifying and eliminating redundancies. This leanness results in a process of *decompensation* whereby the available capacity to keep pace with the changing tempo of events is quickly exhausted. Accordingly, disruptions end up having the effect of increasing the potential for cascades across multiple sectors, because planning within any given sector underemphasizes how interdependencies across infrastructure sectors produces bottlenecks during disruptions. When individual sectors are operating at or above their design capacity, their capability to anticipate, keep pace with, and stay ahead of cascades is limited.

Reversing this decompensation trend requires new market-based incentives that help advance the value proposition for investing in resilience. In the end, the only resilience metrics that matter are the ones that financial and insurance sectors are willing to embrace and provide economic incentives to support. But the finance and insurance sectors have been largely sidelined from playing this role because of the unintended consequence of a growing trend whereby the U.S. government increasingly compensates large infrastructure owners for their losses in the aftermath of disaster.

From 1970 to 2012, 12 of the costliest insured catastrophes worldwide took place after 2000, with three of the top four taking place since 2005. Over that same time, U.S. federal presidential disaster declarations have seen a fivefold increase. Most importantly, the proportion of total loss paid by the federal government for disaster damages has grown from 23% for Hurricane Hugo in 1989 to 80% for Hurricane Sandy in 2012. Meanwhile, the time required to gain congressional approval for disaster assistance has gone from three days after Hurricane Katrina to three months after Hurricane Sandy.

Getting from where we are to where we need to be will require overcoming three barriers that hinder more effective private-public partnerships in advancing regional lifeline infrastructure resilience:

- A lack of agreed-upon metrics to calibrate rewards for undertaking resilience measures.

- The perceptual and behavioral responses that work against owners and operators adequately investing in mitigating measures that can significantly reduce losses for foreseeable disruptive events.

- The moral hazard arising from ever-growing levels of financial relief by the federal government when major disasters occur.

What is required are new incentives that promote resilience that are supported by resilience metrics that relate critical infrastructure performance, operations, and management to market-based return on investment.

The financial and insurance sectors could play an important role in overcoming these barriers by generating a new value proposition for enhancing infrastructure resilience. Specifically, finance and insurance can:

- Inform and focus attention on risks.

- Create incentives for measures that mitigate those risks.

- Provide funds that support the adoption of resilience designs.

- Quickly provide funds as insurance payouts that support rapid recovery when disasters occur.

The role insurance might play in incentivizing the resilience depends on enhanced *risk assessments*, an understanding of *risk perception*, and credible *risk management* that can be analyzed and measured. Absent effective metrics, insurance is likely to be prohibitively costly as insurers seek to reduce their exposure to unexpected losses.

Risk assessment means evaluating the likelihoods and consequences of prospective risks, either by the use of frequency data or on the basis of expert judgments, scenarios, and subjective probabilities. It is important to note that in highly interdependent systems characteristic of regional lifeline infrastructure, failures associated with disasters can propagate rapidly through the system in ways that are not always obvious ex ante.

Risk perception is concerned with the psychological and emotional aspects of risks, which have been shown to have an enormous impact on individual and group behavior. Studies by psychologists have shown that hazards that are least known, are uncontrollable, have catastrophic potential, and are highly dreaded are perceived by the public as being the riskiest. Risk perception has important implications for the effectiveness of alternative policies, most of which are intended to alter aspects of individual and corporate behavior. For example, the systematic misperception of risks affects the willingness to pay for insurance and therefore can erode the effectiveness of insurance as an economic incentive for advancing mitigation measures that enhance critical infrastructure resilience.

Risk management involves developing strategies typically undertaken within both the public and private sectors and seeks to reduce the probabilities of negative events and/or their consequences should they occur. Risk management usually involves investment and the allocation of limited resources that is guided by the assessments of risks and what we know of how people and firms perceive and react to them. In a highly interdependent system where underinvestment in mitigation is typical, an important aspect of risk management is to calibrate just what are the appropriate levels of investment, then identifying ways to encourage that investment. These include policy tools to complement insurance and other risk-transfer mechanisms such as subsidies or tax breaks to encourage early adoption, third-party inspections and audits, and well-enforced regulations and standards.

5.3.3 New Governance Structure

A third overarching imperative to advancing the future of critical infrastructure resilience is that we must devise new governance structures. These structures must be able to successfully navigate financial and legal constraints for wide adoption by local and regional critical infrastructure end users and stakeholders. They also must support advancing organizational capacities and strategies for helping move stakeholders from non-resilient behaviors to resilience-promoting behaviors:

> *Responsiveness vs. routine decision-making*: The ability to decide on and
>   deploy actions to better manage disturbances as they grow and cascade

is critical to resilient performance. Organizational decision processes that work well under normal conditions usually are too slow—marked by stale assessments and late responses—to keep up with the demands that emerge when cascades begin and grow. Planning tends to under-emphasize the extent to which there are interdependencies across multiple infrastructure sectors. What is needed is an enhanced capacity for private and public decision makers to respond to dynamic, high-stakes situations, in the face of considerable uncertainty and significant time constraints.

Synchronization across units vs. working at cross-purposes: The ability to coordinate and synchronize the activities of different groups across multiple jurisdictions and infrastructure sectors in the face of multiple hazards is critical to resilient performance. Without that ability, indi-vidual units act in ways that are locally adaptive, but globally maladap-tive. Working at cross-purposes arises when each group works hard to achieve the local goals defined for their scope of responsibility, but these activities make it more difficult for other groups to meet the responsibilities of their roles or undermine the global or long-term goals that all groups recognize are important. Governance approaches must be devised to overcome the tendency for fragmentation across organizational and jurisdictional boundaries. Future large-scale events will always be different from ones planned for or practiced previously. Senior decision makers must be supported with mechanisms that boost their capacity for synchronizing multiple groups when timely actions are required in the face of uncertainty.

Proactive learning vs. getting stuck in outdated behaviors: As the pace of change grows, previously adaptive strategies are no longer effective or are becoming less effective at coping with old and new threats. Networks with newly embedded technologies are becoming more sprawling, resulting in extensive and often hidden interdependencies. One consequence is the heightened risk of widespread breakdowns following events that previously had only localized fallout. Resilient performance depends on the ability to continually learn and revise policies, plans, and practices to keep up with effects of a dynamic threat landscape. Critically, this capacity to learn is proactive, that is, it picks up early signals that current approaches may be inadequate for meeting new challenges. Proactive learning breaks down when groups discount evidence of increasing brittleness of systems and plans. Proactive learning is critical to sustaining resilient performance as changes occur and new information accumulates and require gover-nance processes that are capable of resisting the pressure to discount evidence that current approaches are inadequate and instead embrace the need for constant modifications in behaviors and actions in order to enhance resilient performance.

Four activities must be undertaken to enhance governance structures:

- *Promote collaboration and coordination* for addressing multiple risks across interdependent lifeline infrastructure sectors that, in turn, involve multiple political actors and legal jurisdictions.

- *Measure performance* in coping with changing infrastructure and environmental conditions by stakeholders and decision makers in diverse governance settings, including regional planning and economic development, risk prevention, infrastructure design and operation, public safety, and emergency management.

- *Recommend* behavioral and organization changes that enhance resilience by improving performance on sensing, anticipating, adapting, and learning tasks.

- *Transfer experiences and knowledge* across organizational and geographic settings and scales.

This translates into the need to identify and implement changes in workforce training, the design and functioning of institutions, the role of standards and regulations, and knowledge systems in place to better assure the continuity and rapid recovery of lifeline functions and the likelihood that there will be post-disaster adaptation. To generate these capabilities requires understanding how institutions and human behaviors unfold in the context of infrastructure systems and a changing social, economic, and bio-cyber-physical environment.

5.3.4   Enhance and Build Resilience Skills Among Professions

A fourth and final imperative for advancing the future of critical infrastructure resilience is the need to enhance and build resilience skills among profession within the national enterprise. Advancing critical infrastructure resilience requires a quantum leap in national capacity in preparing current and future critical infrastructure practitioners, researchers, engineers/designers, business leaders, and policymakers to tackle the challenges to, and opportunities for, bolstering resilience. This can be accomplished only through an interdisciplinary mix of programs. Enhancing and building resilience skills will also benefit from including an analysis of historical cases in which planning, risk perception and prevention, and disaster management and response were misaligned. These cases can help to identify perceptional, behavioral, economic, legal, and institutional barriers to resilient infrastructure system planning, design, and operation. Most importantly, they can be used to guide and promote better regional governance frameworks that support close collaborations among stakeholders from the public, private, and non-profit sectors, and from different regions to include working across local, state, federal, and international jurisdictions. Special focus should be given to validating robust strategies, that is, those that make good sense under non-stationarity conditions.

5.4   Global Efforts to Promote Resilience

With the increasing realization that conventional risk management frameworks are not foolproof, many nations and agencies across the globe have been pushing the agenda to translate resilience into an operational paradigm. In Chapter 1, we discussed the United States' 2013 *Presidential Policy Directive 21 (PPD-21)*. Below are examples of various efforts happening across the globe to advance greater infrastructure resilience.

5.4.1   100 Resilient Cities

The *100 Resilient Cities (100RC) Initiative*[4] is underwritten by the Rockefeller Foundation with the goal of helping cities around the world become more resilient to the physical, social, and economic challenges that are a growing part of the twenty-first century. The 100RC Initiative supports the creation of chief resilience officers within cities who are encouraged to develop and share innovative resilience practices to not just shocks—earthquakes, fires, floods, and so forth—but also the stresses that weaken the fabric of a city on a day-to-day or cyclical basis. Examples of these stresses include high unemployment, an overtaxed or inefficient public transportation system, endemic violence, or chronic food and water shortages. By addressing both the shocks and the stresses, the 100RC Initiative aims to help communities and societies to become better able to respond to adverse events while concurrently being better able to deliver basic functions in both good times and bad, to all populations.

5.4.2   The Dutch Model of Resilience

In 1953, the surge associated with a massive North Sea storm killed more than 1,600 people, flooded most of the Netherlands, damaged farmlands, and destroyed multiple properties. Immediately afterward, the Netherlands established a commission to decide how to deal with the threat of more storms. The commission devised a plan that was enshrined into law, specifying what level of risk is tolerable.

The "Delta-law" was passed in 1959 and updated with the new "Water Act"[5] in 2009. Under this law, the Netherlands has built an extensive network of dikes, dams, sluices, and levees that makes up the Deltawerken. This network represents an ambitious program to erect protective barriers to reduce the risk of flooding to vulnerable areas. Instead of waiting for 100-year extreme rainfall events, the Dutch have lowered the flood risk to 1 in 4,000 years. The law has been enacted in many parts that requires authorities to hold risk in some parts of the country to 1 in 10,000 years.

An example of such resilient design is the **Maeslantkering**—a Storm Surge Barrier for the Port of Rotterdam. The Maeslantkering was completed in 1997; the innovative design allows two massive floating arms to automatically close off access to the North Sea when computers predict a storm surge of more than three meters. Each arm is roughly the size of the Eiffel Tower, although more than twice as heavy. When they meet, the arms sink into fitted grooves deep underwater, creating a single, massive barrier.

More recently, the Dutch have augmented their protective measures with an adaptive one, collectively known as *Room for the River*.[5] The aim of this $2.85 billion project is "to increase safety and to add spatial quality to the area around the rivers rather than raising the height of flood barriers." [6]

The four goals of this program are:

- **Relocation of dikes**: Dikes are being relocated farther from the river shore. This creates additional space within the floodplain for the river during annual floods.

- **Lower the level of the floodplain**: The floodplain bottom is being dredged to lower its depth, allowing it to hold more flood waters without topping the dikes.

- **Increase the depth of the side channels**: Side channels are being dredged to increase their depth in order to increase the barrier between the river and infrastructures and residents. It will also allow for more water to be directed into these channels to reduce the risk of a breach of the dikes safeguarding infrastructure and residential homes.

- **Construction of open spaces and parks**: These spaces and parks can absorb waters during major flood events to reduce the flood risk for residences and critical facilities.

- **Modification or removal of obstacles**: Groins are being modified and obstacles along the river which might retain receding flood waters will be removed.

By blending protective and adaptive measures together, the Netherlands is providing an innovative model for how societies can adapt to a changing climate in ways that advance their overall resilience.

5.4.3   United Kingdom and Resilience Practices

The United Kingdom has also embraced resilience as a national imperative, embedding it in both legal frameworks and official strategic guidance. Two such examples include:

1. The **2004 Civil Contingencies Act (CCA)**[7] calls for an increase in the resilience of society to disasters. The approach includes:
   - Large use of science to support policy
   - Attention to business-continuity issues and full partnerships with the private sector
   - Flexible institutional mechanisms and partnerships focused on delivery through voluntary approaches

- Establishment of local resilience forums to get necessary stakeholders involved at the local level
- National commitment to continue improving policy-making and pushing further implementation.

2. The **2010 National Security Strategy**[8] sets out the objective of "ensuring a secure and resilient United Kingdom: protecting our people, economy, infrastructure, territory and way of life from all major risk that can affect us directly." This includes to:
    - Ensure that disaster risk reduction is a national and local priority with a strong institutional basis for implementation.
    - Identify, assess, and monitor disaster risks and enhance early warning.
    - Use knowledge, innovation, and education to build a culture of safety and resilience at all levels.
    - Reduce underlying risk factors.
    - Strengthen disaster preparedness for effective response at all levels.

5.4.4   UN International Strategy for Disaster Risk Reduction

The United Nations has recently incorporated resilience into two major initiatives: the R!SE initiative and the Making Cities Resilient Campaign.

R!SE—Disaster Risk-Sensitive Investments

The overall goal of the initiative is to make all investments risk-sensitive. R!SE,[9] a UN initiative, will facilitate the exchange of experience and knowledge to implement tangible disaster risk reduction projects through eight streams of activities:

- Strategies for global business

- Risk metrics for economic forecasting

- Industry sector certification

- Education

- Principles for responsible investing

- Resilience of cities

- Insurance

- Resilience of United Nations programming.

Making Cities Resilient Campaign

The Making Cities Resilient[10] campaign addresses issues of local governance and urban risk while drawing upon previous United Nations Office for Disaster Risk Reduction (UNISDR) campaigns on safer schools and hospitals, as well as on the sustainable urbanizations principles developed in the UN-Habitat World Urban Campaign 2009–2013. The *Hyogo Framework for Action 2005–2015: Building the Resilience of Nations and Communities to Disasters*[11] offers solutions for local governments and actors to manage and reduce urban risk. Urban risk reduction provides opportunities for capital investments through infrastructure upgrades and improvements, building retrofits for energy efficiency and safety, urban renovation and renewal, cleaner energies, and slum upgrading. Local governments are the closest level to the citizens and to their communities. They play the first role in responding to crises and emergencies. They deliver essential services to their citizens (health, education, transport, water, etc.), which need to be made resilient to disasters.

To reinforce the above discussion of the policy dimensions associated with advancing critical infrastructure resilience, we provide an exercise that helps to illustrate how stakeholders and policymakers should weigh various factors when making resilience related decisions. Importantly, these considerations incorporate the cost of regret associated with decisions of actions or inactions for adaptation.

5.5   Exercise

In the article "Evaluating Flood Resilience Strategies for Coastal Megacities," Aerts et al.[12] developed a multidisciplinary scientific approach to evaluate flood management strategies. In the paper, the authors discuss the following strategies to reduce vulnerability or avoid flooding or a combination of both for New York City:

S: Storm surge barriers

- Sa: Three barriers to close off pairs of NYC and NJ that preserve wetland dynamics.
- Sb: Barrier that closes off Jamaica Bay "NJ-NY" connect.
- Sc: One large barrier on outer harbor to reduce the length of coastline of New York City.

Hybrid solution: Combining clusters of measures to enhance building code strategies in NYC by elevating, dry or wet floodproofing both existing and new buildings to reduce economic loss due to business interruption. Based on the information given in Table 5.1 and your own analysis, comment on the viability of various strategies. What are the various factors, in addition to financial considerations, you took into account to reach the decision?

Cost breakdown for strategies	Sa	Sb	Sc	Hybrid
Total investment	$21 million	$20 million	$12 million	$11 million
Maintenance	$98.5 million	$126 million	$117.5 million	$13.5 million
Expected benefits (current climate)	$11.45 million	$30.66 million	$48 million	$13.5 million
Expected benefits (future climate)	$157 million	$187 million	$268 million	$49 million

Table 5.1. Breakdown of costs and benefits for various strategies

Suggested reading: Evaluating Flood Resilience Strategies for Coastal Megacities[12]

5.6   Conclusion

Critical infrastructure resilience, on the policy side, needs to balance the diverse perspectives and priorities of stakeholders, regulatory agencies, owners and operators, users and impacted communities, and decision makers at tactical, operational, and strategic levels. Furthermore, infrastructure owners and operators as well as facility managers need to balance multiple objective functions of key players, based on various jurisdictional, functional, political, governance, and organizational structures. The primary drivers of resilience are economic incentive structures, including insurance schemes and financial instruments such as catastrophe bonds. Infrastructure governance need to account for multidimensional jurisdictional structures as well as the need for interinstitutional coordination. Thus, a port authority (as an example of a large-scale infrastructure owner and operator) typically needs to worry about resilience within their enterprise (i.e., systems directly under their supervision) as well as coordinate with external stakeholders (e.g., passenger and freight transport, power utilities, water distribution systems, and communication network companies). Qualitative and quantitative tools, as well as coordination of human stakeholders, are necessary to enable successful policy approaches.

References

[1] National Research Council. Sustainable Critical Infrastructure Systems: a Framework for Meeting 21st Century Imperatives: Report of a Workshop. *National Academies Press* 2009. https://doi.org/10.17226/12638.

[2] NIAC Critical Infrastructure Resilience: Final Report and Recommendations | Homeland Security; n.d. www.dhs.gov/publication/niac-critical-infrastructure-resilience-final-report (accessed August 29, 2017).

[3] National Research Council. Sustainable Critical Infrastructure Systems: a Framework for Meeting 21st Century Imperatives: Report of a Workshop. *National Academies Press* 2009. https://doi.org/10.17226/12638.

[4] 100 Resilient Cities. *Rockefeller Foundation* 2017. http://www.100resilient cities.org/ (accessed December 4, 2017).

[5] Ministry of Transport, Public Works, and Water Management. Water Act. *Government of the Netherlands* 2009.

[6] ClimateWire. "How the Dutch Make 'Room for the River' by Redesigning Cities," *Scientific American.* (January 20, 2012). https://www.scientific american.com/article/how-the-dutch-make-room-for-the-river/ (accessed December 4, 2017).

[7] Civil Contingencies Act 2004, c. 36. https://www.legislation.gov.uk/ukpga/2004/36/pdfs/ukpga_20040036_en.pdf (accessed December 4, 2017).

[8] Great Britain: Cabinet Office. A Strong Britain in an Age of Uncertainty: The National Security Strategy. *The Stationery Office* 2010. https://www.gov.uk/government/publications/the-national-security-strategy-a-strong-britain-in-an-age-of-uncertainty (accessed December 4, 2017).

[9] R!SE Disaster Risk-Sensitive Investments | Program Summary. *United Nations* 2014. http://193.239.220.65/rise/sites/default/files/R%21SE%20 Program%20Summary%20V2.pdf (accessed December 4, 2017).

[10] Making Cities Resilience. *United Nations Office for Disaster Risk Reduction* 2015. https://www.unisdr.org/campaign/resilientcities/ (accessed December 4, 2017).

[11] Hyogo Framework for Action 2005-2015: Building the Resilience of Nations and Communities to Disasters. *United Nations Office for Disaster Risk Reduction* 2007. http://www.unisdr.org/files/1037_hyogoframe workforactionenglish.pdf (accessed December 4, 2007).

[12] Aerts, J.C.J.H., Botzen, W.J.W., Emanuel, K., Lin, N., de Moel, H., Michel-Kerjan, E. O. Evaluating flood resilience strategies for coastal megacities. *Science* 2014;344:473–5. https://doi.org/10.1126/science.1248222.

Appendix

Standard Normal Probabilities

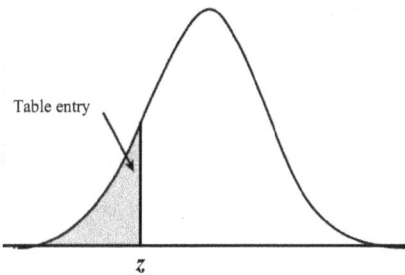

Table entry

Table entry for z is the area under the standard normal curve to the left of z.

z	.00	.01	.02	.03	.04	.05	.06	.07	.08	.09
-3.4	.0003	.0003	.0003	.0003	.0003	.0003	.0003	.0003	.0003	.0002
-3.3	.0005	.0005	.0005	.0004	.0004	.0004	.0004	.0004	.0004	.0003
-3.2	.0007	.0007	.0006	.0006	.0006	.0006	.0006	.0005	.0005	.0005
-3.1	.0010	.0009	.0009	.0009	.0008	.0008	.0008	.0008	.0007	.0007
-3.0	.0013	.0013	.0013	.0012	.0012	.0011	.0011	.0011	.0010	.0010
-2.9	.0019	.0018	.0018	.0017	.0016	.0016	.0015	.0015	.0014	.0014
-2.8	.0026	.0025	.0024	.0023	.0023	.0022	.0021	.0021	.0020	.0019
-2.7	.0035	.0034	.0033	.0032	.0031	.0030	.0029	.0028	.0027	.0026
-2.6	.0047	.0045	.0044	.0043	.0041	.0040	.0039	.0038	.0037	.0036
-2.5	.0062	.0060	.0059	.0057	.0055	.0054	.0052	.0051	.0049	.0048
-2.4	.0082	.0080	.0078	.0075	.0073	.0071	.0069	.0068	.0066	.0064
-2.3	.0107	.0104	.0102	.0099	.0096	.0094	.0091	.0089	.0087	.0084
-2.2	.0139	.0136	.0132	.0129	.0125	.0122	.0119	.0116	.0113	.0110
-2.1	.0179	.0174	.0170	.0166	.0162	.0158	.0154	.0150	.0146	.0143

z	.00	.01	.02	.03	.04	.05	.06	.07	.08	.09
-2.0	.0228	.0222	.0217	.0212	.0207	.0202	.0197	.0192	.0188	.0183
-1.9	.0287	.0281	.0274	.0268	.0262	.0256	.0250	.0244	.0239	.0233
-1.8	.0359	.0351	.0344	.0336	.0329	.0322	.0314	.0307	.0301	.0294
-1.7	.0446	.0436	.0427	.0418	.0409	.0401	.0392	.0384	.0375	.0367
-1.6	.0548	.0537	.0526	.0516	.0505	.0495	.0485	.0475	.0465	.0455
-1.5	.0668	.0655	.0643	.0630	.0618	.0606	.0594	.0582	.0571	.0559
-1.4	.0808	.0793	.0778	.0764	.0749	.0735	.0721	.0708	.0694	.0681
-1.3	.0968	.0951	.0934	.0918	.0901	.0885	.0869	.0853	.0838	.0823
-1.2	.1151	.1131	.1112	.1093	.1075	.1056	.1038	.1020	.1003	.0985
-1.1	.1357	.1335	.1314	.1292	.1271	.1251	.1230	.1210	.1190	.1170
-1.0	.1587	.1562	.1539	.1515	.1492	.1469	.1446	.1423	.1401	.1379
-0.9	.1841	.1814	.1788	.1762	.1736	.1711	.1685	.1660	.1635	.1611
-0.8	.2119	.2090	.2061	.2033	.2005	.1977	.1949	.1922	.1894	.1867
-0.7	.2420	.2389	.2358	.2327	.2296	.2266	.2236	.2206	.2177	.2148
-0.6	.2743	.2709	.2676	.2643	.2611	.2578	.2546	.2514	.2483	.2451
-0.5	.3085	.3050	.3015	.2981	.2946	.2912	.2877	.2843	.2810	.2776
-0.4	.3446	.3409	.3372	.3336	.3300	.3264	.3228	.3192	.3156	.3121
-0.3	.3821	.3783	.3745	.3707	.3669	.3632	.3594	.3557	.3520	.3483
-0.2	.4207	.4168	.4129	.4090	.4052	.4013	.3974	.3936	.3897	.3859
-0.1	.4602	.4562	.4522	.4483	.4443	.4404	.4364	.4325	.4286	.4247
-0.0	.5000	.4960	.4920	.4880	.4840	.4801	.4761	.4721	.4681	.4641

Standard Normal Probabilities

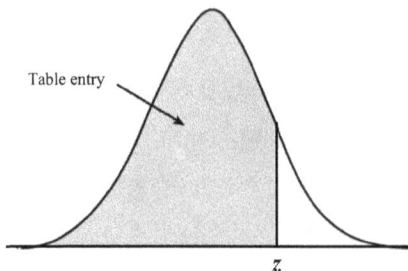

Table entry

Table entry for z is the area under the standard normal curve to the left of z.

z	.00	.01	.02	.03	.04	.05	.06	.07	.08	.09
0.0	.5000	.5040	.5080	.5120	.5160	.5199	.5239	.5279	.5319	.5359
0.1	.5398	.5438	.5478	.5517	.5557	.5596	.5636	.5675	.5714	.5753
0.2	.5793	.5832	.5871	.5910	.5948	.5987	.6026	.6064	.6103	.6141
0.3	.6179	.6217	.6255	.6293	.6331	.6368	.6406	.6443	.6480	.6517
0.4	.6554	.6591	.6628	.6664	.6700	.6736	.6772	.6808	.6844	.6879
0.5	.6915	.6950	.6985	.7019	.7054	.7088	.7123	.7157	.7190	.7224
0.6	.7257	.7291	.7324	.7357	.7389	.7422	.7454	.7486	.7517	.7549
0.7	.7580	.7611	.7642	.7673	.7704	.7734	.7764	.7794	.7823	.7852
0.8	.7881	.7910	.7939	.7967	.7995	.8023	.8051	.8078	.8106	.8133
0.9	.8159	.8186	.8212	.8238	.8264	.8289	.8315	.8340	.8365	.8389
1.0	.8413	.8438	.8461	.8485	.8508	.8531	.8554	.8577	.8599	.8621
1.1	.8643	.8665	.8686	.8708	.8729	.8749	.8770	.8790	.8810	.8830
1.2	.8849	.8869	.8888	.8907	.8925	.8944	.8962	.8980	.8997	.9015
1.3	.9032	.9049	.9066	.9082	.9099	.9115	.9131	.9147	.9162	.9177
1.4	.9192	.9207	.9222	.9236	.9251	.9265	.9279	.9292	.9306	.9319
1.5	.9332	.9345	.9357	.9370	.9382	.9394	.9406	.9418	.9429	.9441
1.6	.9452	.9463	.9474	.9484	.9495	.9505	.9515	.9525	.9535	.9545
1.7	.9554	.9564	.9573	.9582	.9591	.9599	.9608	.9616	.9625	.9633
1.8	.9641	.9649	.9656	.9664	.9671	.9678	.9686	.9693	.9699	.9706
1.9	.9713	.9719	.9726	.9732	.9738	.9744	.9750	.9756	.9761	.9767
2.0	.9772	.9778	.9783	.9788	.9793	.9798	.9803	.9808	.9812	.9817
2.1	.9821	.9826	.9830	.9834	.9838	.9842	.9846	.9850	.9854	.9857
2.2	.9861	.9864	.9868	.9871	.9875	.9878	.9881	.9884	.9887	.9890
2.3	.9893	.9896	.9898	.9901	.9904	.9906	.9909	.9911	.9913	.9916
2.4	.9918	.9920	.9922	.9925	.9927	.9929	.9931	.9932	.9934	.9936
2.5	.9938	.9940	.9941	.9943	.9945	.9946	.9948	.9949	.9951	.9952
2.6	.9953	.9955	.9956	.9957	.9959	.9960	.9961	.9962	.9963	.9964
2.7	.9965	.9966	.9967	.9968	.9969	.9970	.9971	.9972	.9973	.9974

z	.00	.01	.02	.03	.04	.05	.06	.07	.08	.09
2.8	.9974	.9975	.9976	.9977	.9977	.9978	.9979	.9979	.9980	.9981
2.9	.9981	.9982	.9982	.9983	.9984	.9984	.9985	.9985	.9986	.9986
3.0	.9987	.9987	.9987	.9988	.9988	.9989	.9989	.9989	.9990	.9990
3.1	.9990	.9991	.9991	.9991	.9992	.9992	.9992	.9992	.9993	.9993
3.2	.9993	.9993	.9994	.9994	.9994	.9994	.9994	.9995	.9995	.9995
3.3	.9995	.9995	.9995	.9996	.9996	.9996	.9996	.9996	.9996	.9997
3.4	.9997	.9997	.9997	.9997	.9997	.9997	.9997	.9997	.9997	.9998

Index

Note: Page numbers in italic indicate a figure and page numbers in bold indicate a table on the corresponding page.

For Product Safety Concerns and Information please contact our EU
representative GPSR@taylorandfrancis.com
Taylor & Francis Verlag GmbH, Kaufingerstraße 24, 80331 München, Germany